THE
MAGNIFICAT READERS

SECOND READER

ST. AUGUSTINE ACADEMY PRESS
HOMER GLEN, IL

All textual content found herein has been taken from approved
Catholic sources (having an imprimatur or other ecclesiastical approval)
or, in the case of some poems and sheet music, material used was
textually identical to copies found in approved sources.

With some exceptions, all sources used for this compilation
are public domain; where this is not the case,
fair use doctrine has been carefully observed.

This compilation is based on the recommended readings
for each grade level as published in the *Religion in Life Curriculum*,
published by the Marquette University
Institute of Catechetical Research between 1933-1935.
Additional selections of interest were added from the same sources.

This compilation ©2018 by St. Augustine Academy Press.
Edited by Lisa Bergman.

Softcover ISBN: 978-1-64051-025-8

Contents

A Child's Morning Prayer..........................*Mary L. Duncan* 1
Rosary Reader 2
Three Little Rules..*S. G. Stern* 2
Rosary Reader 2
Why the Birds Sing.. 3
Ideal Catholic Reader 2
The Bird's Prayer... 4
Ideal Catholic Reader 2
A Child's Prayer.................................*M. Betham Edwards* 5
American Reader 2
A Little Boy's Prayer.. 6
American Reader 2
Mozart's Prayer.. 9
American Reader 2
Little Samuel... 13
Cathedral Basic Reader 2
How Ruth Found Her Way.. 17
American Cardinal Reader 2
A Gift..*Mary Dixon Thayer* 21
Misericordia Reader 2
Blessed Herman-Joseph..........................*Catholic Folklore* 22
Misericordia Reader 2
The First Day of School... 27
Marywood Reader 2
The Baby....................................*George MacDonald* 32
The Story of the King.. 34
Life on Earth of Our Blessed Lord
Whose Birthday Was Best?.. 35
American Cardinal Reader 2
The Chosen One.. 39
The Catholic Child 2
Who Made the Bird?.. 42
American Reader 2
The Creator ....*Cecil Frances Alexander* 45
American Reader 2

God's Outdoors.. 46
American Cardinal Reader 2
God's Light... 48
Ideal Catholic Reader 2
I Wish I Could See the Bright Angel........*Mary E. Mannix* 49
When Little Children Wake at Morn......*Mary E. Mannix* 51
The Law Which God Gave... 52
Life on Earth of Our Blessed Lord
The Law is Broken.. 52
Life on Earth of Our Blessed Lord
A Child's Thought at Christmas................*Mary Jane Carr* 54
The Blessed Virgin................*Henry Wadsworth Longfellow* 55
Child of Nazareth........................*Rev. John Banister Tabb* 56
A Love Song...............................*Charles L. O'Donnell, C.S.C.* 57
Like One I Know ....*Nancy Campbell* 58
A Little Child at the Crib... 59
Jesus Answers From the Crib.........*Rev. Michael Earls, S.J.* 60
Presents..*Mary Dixon Thayer* 62
Gifts..*Julia Davis* 63
Rosary Reader 2
The Toy Train.. 64
Ideal Catholic Reader 2
The King's Highway............................*Rev. Hugh F. Blunt* 68
Mary, Mother of God ......*from The Little Catholic's Choral* 70
The Boyhood of Jesus.. 73
Ideal Catholic Reader 2
The Christ Child..*G. K. Chesterton* 75
American Cardinal Reader 2
A Mother's Quest..................................*Rev. Hugh F. Blunt* 76
Ideal Catholic Reader 4
The Annunciation... 78
American Reader 2
The Baptism of Jesus... 80
Life on Earth of Our Blessed Lord
The Children of the King.. 81
Marywood Reader 2

Speak Little Voice............................*Rev. Michael Earls, S.J.* 83
Cathedral Basic Reader 2
The Old Woman and the Cakes.. 84
An Honest Boy.. 87
Ideal Catholic Reader 2
The Temptation of Jesus... 89
Life on Earth of Our Blessed Lord
St. Peter's Answer.. 90
Life on Earth of Our Blessed Lord
The Calling of Saint Matthew.. 91
Rosary Reader 2
Mother Dear, Pray for Me... 93
De La Salle Hymnal
The Lord's First Miracle... 94
Life on Earth of Our Blessed Lord
Finding You..*Mary Dixon Thayer* 95
The Helper..*Rev. Hugh F. Blunt* 97
A Bunch of Golden Keys... 97
Practical Aids for Catholic Teachers
Little Things......................*Father Frederick William Faber* 99
What Have I?...*Christina Rossetti* 100
Our Lord Cures the Lame Man...................................... 101
Misericordia Reader 1
Holy God, We Praise Thy Name..................................... 105
The Making of Birds..................*Katharine Tynan Hinkson* 106
The Rich Ruler's Daughter... 108
Marquette Reader 2
The Kindness of Jesus.. 111
Ideal Catholic Reader 2
The Daughter of Jairus... 112
Life on Earth of Our Blessed Lord
The Poor Widow's Son.. 112
Life on Earth of Our Blessed Lord
Night and Day...*Mary Mapes Dodge* 113
Marquette Reader 2
The Storm... 114
Marquette Reader 2

Saint Valentine.. 116
The Catholic Child 2
Jesus, Tender Shepherd... 118
Sheep and Lambs.....................*Katharine Tynan Hinkson* 119
The Shepherdess...*Alice Meynell* 120
I Will Follow Thee.. 122
Excelsior Reader 2
The Lamb...*William Blake* 124
Marquette Reader 2
The Good Shepherd... 125
Every Child's Garden
The Good Shepherd... 127
American Cardinal Reader 2
A Useful Lesson.............................*Rev. M. Russell, S.J.* 130
My Neighbor...............................*Rev. John Banister Tabb* 130
The Lowest Place................................*Christina Rossetti* 131
Come to Jesus...................*Father Frederick William Faber* 132
Discontent...*Sarah Orne Jewett* 135
The Very Time................................*Mary Dixon Thayer* 137
The Prodigal Son.. 138
Rosary Reader 2
The Load of Wood... 140
Rosary Reader 2
A Child's Evening Prayer..........*Samuel Taylor Coleridge* 144
Different Ways..................................*Mary Dixon Thayer* 145
A Prayer to Mary..................................*Rev. H.G. Hughes* 146
Thoughts..*Mary Dixon Thayer* 147
A Prayer.. 148
Cathedral Reader 3
The Lord's Prayer... 149
The Catholic Child 1
Triumphal Hymn for Palm Sunday *Trans. D.J. Donahoe* 150
Shields Catholic Education Series Book 3
Blessed Candle.............................*Joseph Kinney Collins* 152
Communion..*Caroline Giltinian* 153

After a Visit to the Blessed Sacrament......*S.M. St. John* 154
A Child's Wish................................*Rev. Abram J. Ryan* 155
Ideal Catholic Reader 2
Blessed Imelda.. 157
American Cardinal Reader 2
St. Cyril... 162
American Cardinal Reader 2
A Lover of Children... 166
American Reader 2
The First Communion.. 170
Life on Earth of Our Blessed Lord
The Wonderful Gift.. 171
The Catholic Child 2
O Lord I Am Not Worthy (*O Sacrament Most Holy*)...... 172
De La Salle Hymnal
The Child on Calvary................*Rev. John Banister Tabb* 173
Practical Aids for Catholic Teachers
Nails..*Rev. Leonard Feeney, S.J.* 174
He is Risen.. 177
Ideal Catholic Reader 2
The First Easter.. 178
Rosary Reader 2
The Resurrection... 180
Life on Earth of Our Blessed Lord
Frank's First Confession.. 181
Ideal Catholic Reader 2
O Come Holy Spirit.. 184
Misericordia Reader 1
Come, Holy Ghost.. 185
De La Salle Hymnal
Saint Peter.. 186
Rosary Reader 1
Long Live the Pope.. 190
St. Gregory Hymnal
Saint Felix and the Spider......................*Catholic Folklore* 192
Misericordia Reader 1
Jerome and the Lion...............................*Catholic Folklore* 197
Misericordia Reader 1

The String of Beads... 207
Rosary Reader 2
Playing Saints.. 210
Rosary Reader 2
Mary's Smile... 212
Rosary Reader 2
Sleep Song........................*Denis A. McCarthy* 214
Rosary Reader 2

A Child's Morning Prayer

I thank Thee, Lord, for quiet rest,
  And for Thy care of me;
Oh, let me through this day be blest
  And kept from harm by Thee.

—*Mary L. Duncan*

Three Little Rules

Three little rules we all should keep
 To make life happy and bright;
Smile in the morning; smile at noon;
 And keep on smiling at night!

—*S. G. Stern*

Why the Birds Sing

Last summer, little John White spent ten weeks in the country with his grandpa and his grandma.

Like every little boy, he saw a great many things that he did not understand.

One morning, John got up very early.

But the little birds were up before him.

They were singing on the tree near his window.

When grandpa got up, little John ran to him and said: "Grandpa, why do the birds sing so early in the morning, before they have their breakfast?"

"Now, John, don't you say your morning prayers before breakfast?"

"Yes, grandpa; I do."

"That is what the little birds do, when they sing early in the morning. They praise God in their way."

The Bird's Prayer

"Pretty little song bird,
    Happy as a king,
Will you tell me truly
    Why is it you sing?"

"Early in the morning,
    At the break of day,
High up in the blue sky,
    In sweet tones I pray.

"I praise God the Father
    Every time I sing;
I then pay my homage
    To the Great High King."

A Child's Prayer

God make my life a little light,
   Within the world to glow;
A tiny flame that burneth bright
   Wherever I may go.

God make my life a little flower,
   That giveth joy to all,
Content to bloom in native bower,
   Although its place be small.

God make my life a little song,
   That comforteth the sad;
That helpeth others to be strong,
   And makes the singer glad.

—M. Betham Edwards

A Little Boy's Prayer

"Joseph dear, it is time that you were in bed," said Mrs. Little.

"Very well, mother; I will go at once."

Joseph said "Good Night" to his father and his mother, and went to his room.

Sometime later, Mrs. Little went upstairs to see if her son was in bed.

She found him saying his prayers.

Dressed in his pretty white pajamas, he was kneeling near his bed.

What prayer do you think he was saying?

Would you like to know?

This is what he said:

"Good night, dear Lord, good night.

"Mother told me that it was time for me to be in bed.

"I feel tired and sleepy.

"I have played all day with my toys and my games,

"I know that I had a good time.

"I thank you, dear Lord, for Your kindness to me.

"Good night again, dear Lord.

"Please do not forget to send an angel to care for me while I sleep.

"You know, dear Lord, that I do not like the dark.

"I want an angel near me.

"When the angel is in the room, I will not be afraid of the dark.

"Tell the angel to stay with me all the night.

"I am only a little boy.

"I need his care.

"The angel will protect me.

"He will keep me from danger.

"He will help me to be good.

"He will stay awake while I sleep.

"Good night, dear Lord, good night."

Mozart and his sister at the Piano by Hermann Schneider

Mozart's Prayer

Many years ago, two dear little children, a boy and a girl, lived in a small house near a large river.

These two children loved music very much.

When the little girl was six years old, she could play the piano.

Her tiny brother, Wolfgang, was even a better player.

Every one that heard him play said he was a wonder.

Just as these children were beginning to enjoy life, the times became so hard that they did not always have enough to eat.

One afternoon, Wolfgang and his sister went for a walk.

The boy said to his sister: "Let us take a long walk in the forest. I love to hear the wild birds sing, and to catch the sound of the flowing river. They seem like music to me."

They walked a long way from home. Everything they saw made them think of God Who made this wonderful world.

When the children came to a fallen tree, they rested for a short time.

"This is a good place to pray," said Wolfgang.

"For what shall we pray?"

"Let us pray for father and mother," said Wolfgang.

"Dear mother hardly ever smiles now. Father, too, seems very sad.

"Let us ask God to help them."

The children knelt on the grass and prayed from their hearts.

This is what they said:

"Dear God, please help father and mother to get enough for us to eat; and, dear God, show us how to help them."

"How can we help them?" asked the sister.

"By and by, when I become a man, I shall play before a great many rich persons, and they will give me plenty of money.

"I shall give all the money I get to my father and my mother.

"Then we can live in a beautiful house, and be very happy."

As Wolfgang finished talking, he heard someone laughing.

The boy turned around and saw a gentleman on horseback.

"Good afternoon, children," said the gentleman.

"Good afternoon, sir," replied the children.

The gentleman then asked many, many questions. The little girl answered every one of them.

"What is this little fellow going to be when he becomes a man?" asked the gentleman.

"He hopes to be a great musician," replied the little girl. "Then he can earn much money, and we shall be poor no longer."

"He may do that when he has learned to play well enough," said the gentleman.

"He plays well now, sir."

"No, no; that cannot be," said the gentleman.

"Come and see us, sir, and I shall play for you," said Wolfgang.

"I shall call on you this very evening," said the gentleman.

The children went home and told their father and mother about the gentleman they met in the forest.

Soon someone knocked at the door.

"Come in," said Mr. Mozart.

The door opened and in came a man with a basket of things to eat.

"What does all this mean?" asked Mr. Mozart.

"It means, dear Father, that God heard our prayer."

"What prayer, my child?"

"This afternoon we asked God to help us to get enough to eat; and now, dear Father, He has done so."

Not long after this, while Wolfgang was playing one of his pieces, the gentleman they had met in the forest stood near the open door.

He was so delighted that he invited Mr. Mozart and his family to come and live near him.

He said to the father: "I should like to get the best teachers for Wolfgang. He is a wonderful player."

In a week or two the Mozart family moved near the gentleman's home, and Wolfgang studied very hard every day.

He became a great musician, and everybody loves his beautiful music.

Little Samuel

A long time ago there was a woman named Anna. She had no children, and she wanted a son.

One day Anna went to the temple and prayed. In her prayer she said, "Dear Lord, please give me a son.

"This is my promise. If I have a son, I will give him to You. I will bring him to this temple, and he shall always do Your work."

Anna's prayer was answered. After a time God gave her a son, and she named the child Samuel.

The mother was happy as she cared for her baby. And she did not forget the promise she had made to God. She wanted her son to do God's work.

When little Samuel was old enough, Anna took him to the temple. She told a kind old priest named

Heli about her promise. Then she asked him to take care of her child.

Heli was kind to the boy, and Samuel grew to love him.

Every day the old priest talked to the child about God. He showed Samuel how he could help in the temple.

The boy did all he could to help Heli, and learned to do many things.

One night Samuel had gone to bed. It was almost dark in the temple, but there was a light before the holy place.

As he slept, Samuel heard his name called. He jumped up and ran to the old priest. "Here I am," said the boy. "Did you call me?"

"No," Heli said, "I did not call you. Go back to your bed."

Samuel went back and slept. But soon he heard another call. Again he ran to Heli and said, "Here I am, Father. You called me."

"No, my son," said the priest, "I did not call you. Go back to your bed."

Samuel lay down, but he did not go to sleep. He

was sure that someone had called him. Soon he thought a kind hand lay upon his head. The child was not afraid, but was very, very happy.

Once more a Voice called Samuel. He hurried to the priest, and said, "Yes, Father. I am sure you called me."

Then Heli knew that a Voice from Heaven had called the boy. "Go back to your bed, my son," he said. "The Voice is from Heaven. If you hear it again, say, 'Speak, Lord, for I am listening.'"

Samuel went back, and again he heard the Voice call, "Samuel! Samuel!" The boy knelt down and answered, "Speak, Lord, for I am listening."

Then God talked to Samuel, and the boy listened so well that he remembered every word. The next

morning he went to Heli and told him all that the Lord had said.

After that, Samuel always listened for God's Voice. And God talked to the boy very often.

When Samuel grew older, he became a priest. His people loved him and came to him when they needed help. They knew that the Lord talked with their priest and that Samuel did as God told him.

Even after Samuel became an old man, he talked to God just as a child would talk to Him. Every day when he prayed this old priest said, "Speak, Lord, for am listening."

How Ruth Found Her Way

Ruth and Robert lived with their mother in a house at the edge of the woods.

It was a long walk to the nearest town. The road to it ran through the woods.

Every day Robert went to this town to sell the little cakes his mother made. Sometimes he took fresh eggs to sell, too.

One day Robert was ill and could not go to town. His mother could not go, for she had to take care of him.

Ruth said, "Mother, please let me take the cakes and eggs to town to-day. I have gone there so often with Robert, I am sure I know the way."

Ruth's mother said, "There are many paths in the woods, dear. I am afraid you would not find the right one without Robert's help."

"O, I am sure I know the right path, Mother. Please let me go. Let me try to help you as Robert does," begged Ruth.

Ruth's mother thought for a while. Then she said, "You may go, dear. Your Guardian Angel will take care of you."

The cakes were packed neatly in one basket. The eggs were put into another. Ruth took a basket in each hand and started off.

It took her a long time to reach the town. It took her a long time to sell all the cakes and eggs, too. It was late when she was ready to start for home.

"I must hurry. I want to be home before it is dark," she said to herself.

Ruth ran through the woods as fast as she could. At last she came to a place where two paths met. She did not know which path to follow. It seemed to her that she had never seen this place before.

Ruth thought she was lost but she was not afraid. She knew her Guardian Angel would help her. She prayed,

"Beautiful Angel,
My guardian so mild,
Tenderly guide me,
For I am thy child."

Then she walked along one of the paths.

Before she had gone very far, she saw a big flat rock under one of the trees. "O," she said, "I know now I am on the right path. Robert and I have often rested on that rock, on our way home from town. Thank you, Guardian Angel, for helping me."

Ruth ran along this path. It led her out of the woods and right to her own home.

"I am so glad you are safe at home again, Ruth," said her mother.

"My Guardian Angel took care of me, Mother," said Ruth. Then she told her mother about the two paths in the woods.

A Gift

Take all of me to-day, dear God!
   I want to give You all
I think and do and say and am
   From morning to nightfall!

I want to live for You to-day!
   I want to try to fill
Each minute up with love for You—
   And, oh, I hope I will!

—*Mary Dixon Thayer*

Blessed Herman-Joseph

About seven hundred years ago in the far-off land of France, there lived a dear little boy named Herman.

Herman's mother was very good, and she loved God with all her heart.

As soon as Herman could talk, his mother taught him his prayers. She taught him to make the Sign of the Cross and to say the Our Father and the Hail Mary. Each morning and night little Herman would kneel at his mother's knee and say these beautiful prayers to our dear Lord and His Holy Mother.

By and by Herman was old enough to go to school. Here he tried to be a good boy and to obey the master who taught him to read and to count.

On the way to school each day, Herman passed a church. It was called the Church of St. Mary. In this church there was a large statue of our Blessed Lady holding the little Christ Child in her arms.

Herman loved to stop in the church on his way to school. In the morning he would get up early and, after breakfast, would run all the way to church. There he would go up close to the altar and kneel down and say, "Good morning, dear Jesus in the Blessed Sacrament. I love You. Please make me a good boy."

Then he would go to our Blessed Lady's altar and kneel down to say his morning prayers. As he looked at the statue of Our Lady and the Christ Child, he would think of our Blessed Mother who is in Heaven. He would ask her to take care of him and to pray for him, because he, too, wished to go to Heaven someday.

Then he would say good-bye to our Lord and His Blessed Mother and go to school.

Herman's mother was very poor. One day she said to her little boy, "I have no bread for your dinner to-day, I have no meat and no milk, but here is an apple. If you eat this, you will not be so very hungry, my poor little boy."

"An apple is enough, Mother dear,' said Herman. "I do not mind being poor and having little dinner. Our Blessed Mother and the little Christ Child were poor, too. Perhaps they will love me more because I am poor."

Then Herman kissed his mother and ran off to school. It was early, so he stopped in the Church of St. Mary.

After he had said good morning to our Lord in the Blessed Sacrament, he went to Blessed Mother's altar.

"Dear Mother Mary, I do love you so much," he said. "I wish I had something to give you. I cannot give you my schoolbook, because my master told me to bring it to school."

Then Herman tried to think of something to give to our Blessed Lady. All at once he thought of the apple in his pocket. He took it out and, holding it up, said, "Dear Lady, will you please take my apple? I want you to have it, oh! so much, because I love you and your little Boy."

Then a wonderful thing happened. The statue came to life, and our Blessed Lady put out her hand and took the apple. Then she gave it to the little Lord Jesus whom she held in her arms.

"Thank you, my dear little child," she said. "Because you have given me all you have, I will be your mother always, and my little Son will bless you."

All his life long Herman loved our dear Blessed Mother.

One day, when he was a grown man, he was kneeling in prayer before Our Lady's statue. Again the statue came to life, and Our Lady came down to talk to him.

"Give me your hand, my son," she said. Then she placed a ring upon Herman's finger, saying, "From to-day, you shall always be mine, Herman. Call yourself no longer Herman, but let your name be Herman-Joseph."

And so we know this dear saint by the name of Blessed Herman-Joseph. Let us ask him to pray for us that we, too, may love our Blessed Lady and the little Lord Jesus as he did.

The First Day of School

It was the first day of school.

The bell of Saint Peter's school was ringing.

"Come to school, come to school," said the bell.

The boys and girls hurried along the street.

They were glad to get back to school. Jack did not hurry. He was not glad to go. Jack had never been to Saint Peter's school.

Last year he had gone to Saint Mary's school. Saint Mary's school was in another town. Father and Mother and Jack had moved. Jack had been in the First Grade at Saint Mary's. He liked the First Grade. He liked Saint Mary's school. He knew the Sisters, and they knew him. He knew all the boys and girls.

At Saint Peter's school everything would be new to him. He had been so happy to know that he would be in the Second Grade. Now he was not sure about it.

The bell rang again. Sister was at the door to meet the boys and girls. She said "Good morning" to them.

All the boys and girls said "Good morning" to Sister.

When all the children were in their places, they made the sign of the cross. They said their prayers. Then they had lessons from the catechism. Sister talked to the children.

Then she went around the room and spoke to each one of them. She stopped at Jack's desk. She called him Jack. Jack wondered how she knew his name. Sister talked so kindly to him that Jack felt quite at home.

Jack had brought his card from Saint Mary's school. Sister looked at the card. She saw that Jack had done well in the First Grade.

After Sister had talked to all the boys and

girls, she read a story to them. When playtime came, the boys asked Jack to play with them. They did not let him feel lonely. When Jack went home for lunch, he called to his mother.

"Oh, Mother," he said, "I am sure I shall like Saint Peter's school. Everyone was very kind to me.

Sister says I am to be in the Second Grade. And to-morrow we shall get our new Second Readers."

WHERE DID YOU COME FROM BABY DEAR

The Baby

Where did you come from, baby dear?
Out of the everywhere into the here.

Where did you get your eyes so blue?
Out of the sky as I came through.

What makes the light in them sparkle and spin?
Some of the starry spikes left in.

Where did you get that little tear?
I found it waiting when I got here.

What makes your forehead so smooth and high?
A soft hand stroked it as I went by.

What makes your cheek like a warm white rose?
Something better than any one knows.

Whence that three-cornered smile of bliss?
Three angels gave me at once a kiss.

Where did you get that pearly ear?
God spoke, and it came out to hear.

Where did you get those arms and hands?
Love made itself into hooks and bands.

Feet, whence did you come, you darling things?
From the same box as the cherubs' wings.

How did they all just come to be you?
God thought about me, and so I grew.

But how did you come to us, you dear?
God thought of you, and so I am here.

—*George MacDonald*

The Story of the King

To every little boy and girl,
  This blessed tale is given:
About a King who loved us so
  That He came down from heaven,
And died upon the cross for us,
  So we might know and love
And serve Him ever in this world
  And reign with Him above.

Whose Birthday Was Best?

One night Mother, Father and the children were in the living room. Jean and John were talking about the best time to have a birthday.

John said, "I think it is fine to have a birthday in winter. There is snow to play in then. There is ice to skate on, too. I am glad my birthday comes then."

"I am glad mine comes in the spring," said Jean. "The birds that went south for the winter come back then. Pretty green leaves come out on the trees and bushes. Flowers begin to bloom and there is grass on the ground. I think spring is the best time to have a birthday. Don't you think so, too, Mother?"

Mother said, "Spring and winter are both fine times for birthdays, Jean. I like the time of your birthday. I like the time of John's, too; but I like the time of Baby's birthday best of all."

"I have forgotten when Baby's birthday is, Mother. Please tell me," said John.

"It is September 8," said Mother.

"Why is that such a fine day for a birthday, Mother?" asked Jean.

Jean's mother said, "Long, long ago, before Jesus came from Heaven, a beautiful baby girl was born on September 8. She was born in a country, far, far away. Her mother and father loved God dearly. They wished their little girl to love and serve Him all her life. So while she was still very little, they taught her to pray. They taught her what she must do to please God.

"When this little girl grew older, her parents

brought her to the Temple. There she learned to do the things all girls learned to do then. She learned to spin and weave and sew. She learned to keep a house in order. She learned to read and write, too. In her work she always tried to please God by doing her best.

"Every one who knew her loved her, for she was always gentle, kind and good. She never did anything that was not pleasing to God. She prayed each day that she might do only what God wished her to do.

"After many years God showed her how much He loved her for being so good. He chose her to be the Mother of Jesus."

"O Mother," said Jean, "I know now why September 8 is such a beautiful time for a birthday. It is the birthday of our Blessed Mother."

"Yes, Jean, it is," said Mother.

Then Father said, "We named our baby Mary because she was born on our Blessed Mother's birthday."

"Then I think we should call her Mary and not Baby," said John.

Father, Mother and Jean said they thought so, too. So after that the baby was always called by her own beautiful name—Mary.

The Chosen One

THE PRAYER

A long, long time ago there lived a very holy woman, who was called Anne, and a very good man, whose name was Joachim.

Anne and Joachim prayed to God for many years that He would bless their home with a little child. At last God heard their prayer and sent them a dear little baby girl. They called the baby Mary, which means "Lady."

Anne and Joachim loved little Mary dearly, but they knew that she was a gift from God. So when Mary was three years old, they took her to the Temple and gave her back to God.

For many years Mary lived in the Temple where she learned to love God more and more.

She was very happy to do the work of the Temple because it was the house of God.

MARY GOES TO NAZARETH

When Mary was fourteen, she left the Temple and went to take care of a little house in Nazareth. She had to sweep and bake, and spin and weave. But she did it all for God and so she was very happy.

Mary was so beautiful before God that even the angels liked to be near her.

THE ANGEL COMES TO MARY

One day, when Mary was praying in her little home at Nazareth, she saw a wonderful light, brighter than the sunshine. A beautiful angel stood before her. Mary was afraid.

But the angel said, "Hail, full of grace, the Lord is with thee: Blessed art thou among

women." Then the angel told Mary not to fear for God had chosen her to be the mother of Jesus, the Son of God.

Then with great joy, Mary bowed her head and said, "Be it done to me according to thy word."

From the words the angel spoke to Mary, a beautiful prayer has been made. It is the "Hail Mary."

Mary loves this prayer. You may be sure that she will love and bless you if you say it often.

Who Made the Bird?

"I want to tell you a story, children," said the teacher one morning.

Every child in the room sat up.

"That is right," said the teacher. "Now that all the children are ready, I will begin the story.

"As I was coming to school this morning, I saw a very pretty house.

"On the front of the house near a window, I saw a cage.

"In the cage was a dear little bird.

"The little bird seemed so happy.

"He was singing a wonderful song.

"I did not understand what the bird said, but it was beautiful.

"I never heard a song so sweet.

"Then I began to think why the little bird was so happy.

"Was it because he had a new cage?

"Was it because he was in the sun?

"Was it because he had had a good breakfast?

"It is hard to say why the little bird was happy.

"He did not tell me, so I cannot tell you.

"Who makes these happy little creatures?

"I'm sure you know that God makes them for us.

"Men make many things. They make houses, automobiles, airships, and other wonderful things, but only God can make things that have life.

"He gave life to you, and He gave life to me.

"He gave life to all living things in the world.

"God lives in heaven.

"We cannot see Him, but He can see us. He can see in the dark.

"He sees us all the time.

"He is everywhere.

"He knows all things.

"He cares for us all the time.

"God is a kind and loving Father."

The Creator

All things bright and beautiful,
  All creatures great and small,
All things wise and wonderful, —
  The Lord God made them all.

Each little flower that opens,
  Each little bird that sings,
God made their glowing colors,
  He made their tiny wings.

The cold wind in the winter,
  The pleasant summer sun,
The ripe fruits in the garden,
  He made them every one.

He gave us eyes to see them,
  And lips that we might tell
How great is God Almighty
  Who hath made all things well.

—Cecil Frances Alexander

God's Outdoors

The grass is a beautiful carpet,
  And a vast, blue roof is the sky;
The trees are like huge umbrellas,
  When the sun is hot and high.

The snow is a soft, white blanket,
   Laid on when the days are cold;
And the ice is a clear, bright mirror,
   That winter likes to hold.

To enjoy and love all seasons
   We are not too young or small;
How good is our dear Creator,
   The Lord and Maker of all!

God's Light

It was eight o'clock, and little Clare was going to bed.

Her mamma had just put out the lights, and was about to go downstairs.

Little Clare, you know, did not like to be in the dark.

Just then she saw the bright moon in the sky.

She said to her mamma: "Is the moon God's light?"

"Yes, Clare; the moon and the stars are all God's light."

"Will God blow out His light, and go to sleep, mamma?"

"Oh, no, my dear child; God's wonderful light is always burning, and God never sleeps."

"Oh, then, mamma," said Clare, "I will never again be afraid."

I Wish I Could See the Bright Angel

> I wish I could see the bright angel
>   Who walks all the day by my side.
> I wish I could say to him, "Thank You,"
>   For being my guard and my guide.
>
> —Mary E. Mannix

When Little Children Wake at Morn

When little children wake at morn
   To greet once more the day newborn,
The angels take each tiny hand
   And lead them forth from Slumberland.

When little children laugh and play
   'Mid snares and perils of the day,
The guardian angels stand between
   Each lure and pitfall dark, unseen.

When little children sink to sleep,
   Above them white-winged angels keep
A loving watch from dark to light,
   All through the terrors of the night.

And when in dreams they softly smile
   With hearts and lips that know not guile,
Their souls forsake the haunts of men
   And wander back to heaven again.

—Mary E. Mannix

The Law Which God Gave

Do you know why Christ came to us?
  Because, long years ago,
When God created all the world
  And all the things that grow:
To Adam and Eve, in paradise,
  He said: "That you may live
And never die, there's one command,
  One law which I shall give."

The Law is Broken

"Behold the Tree of Knowledge,
  To try you, there it stands.
Of this you shall not taste the fruit
  Nor touch it with your hands."
First Eve, then Adam, broke the Law,
  That Law which God had made;
So they were sent away from God,
  Because they DISOBEYED.

Adam and Eve driven out of Eden by Gustave Doré

A Child's Thought at Christmas

If little Jesus would come looking for a place
    this winter night,
  For a place to lay His head,
  I should offer him my bed,
And I'd tuck Him in with blankets soft and
    warm and white;
  I should place a rocking chair
  Close beside his pillow, where
Mother Mary dear could rock Him if he'd wake
    and cry;
And for Saint Joseph I should put my daddy's
    chair close by.
—Mary Jane Carr

The Blessed Virgin

If our faith had given us nothing more
  Than this example of all womanhood,
So mild, so merciful, so strong, so good,
  So patient, peaceful, loyal, loving, pure,
This were enough to prove it higher and truer
  Than all the creeds the world had known before.

—*Henry Wadsworth Longfellow*

Child of Nazareth

I.

Once, measuring His height, He stood
   Beneath a cypress-tree,
And, leaning back against the wood,
   Stretched wide His arms for me;
Whereat a brooding mother-dove
Fled fluttering from her nest above.

II.

At evening He loved to walk
Among the shadowy hills and talk
   of Bethlehem.
   But if perchance there passed us by
The paschal lambs, He'd look at them
   In silence, long and tenderly;
And when again He'd try to speak,
I've seen the tears upon His cheek.

—Rev. John Banister Tabb

A Love Song

Always I loved a baby,
   A baby loved to hold.
See, I have stolen a Baby
   Out of a House of Gold.

I found in the Tower of Ivory
   A Little One asleep.
I have carried Him down the mountain.
   He is mine to keep.

His Mother is my Mother,
   His Foster Father my friend,
And I shall have Him and love Him
   World without end.

—Charles L. O'Donnell, C.S.C.

Like One I Know

Little Christ was good, and lay
   Sleeping, smiling in the hay;
Never made the cows' round eyes
   Open wider at His cries;
Never, when the night was dim,
   Startled guardian Seraphim,
Who above Him in the beams
   Kept their watch round His white dreams;
Let the rustling brown mice creep
   Undisturbed about His sleep.
Yet if it had not been so—
   Had He been like one I know,
Fought with little fumbling hands,
   Kicked inside His swaddling bands,
Puckered willful crimsoning face—
   Mary Mother, full of grace,
At that little naughty thing,
   Still had been a-worshipping.

—Nancy Campbell

A Little Child at the Crib

O sweetest Baby Jesus,
   How cold You were that night,
No Santa Claus came near You,
   No candles gave You light.

If I were there, dear Jesus,
   I'd put You in my bed
And wrap You warm, dear Jesus,
   And cover up Your head.

And when You woke, dear Jesus,
   I'd share my toys with You,
And when the tree was lighted,
   You'd clap Your Hands and coo.

But Mother told me, Jesus,
   You did not care to play,
For God, the Father, sent You
   To take our sins away.

And You are our real Santa
   Who gave us more than toys;
For gates of Heaven You opened
   To everlasting joys.
I'll always love You, Jesus,
   And Mary Mother, too,
And, oh, I hope in Heaven
   She'll let me play with You.

Jesus Answers From the Crib

Though I am but a Baby,
   I understand your prayer;
For I am God, My dearest,
   And I love your soul, so fair.

For Mother Mary told Me,
    As she kissed Me goodnight,
How much she loved your promise
    To make My Christmas bright.

The little stars were candles,
    And angels sang with glee,
When I was born at Christmas
    So far across the sea.

My cradle was a manger;
    My nursery was a stall;
But I was there, your Jesus,
    And Mary, Queen of all.

Now, Merry Christmas, dearest,
    And when your life is through,
In Heaven I'll be your Santa
    And share My toys with you.

—Rev. Michael Earls, S. J.

Presents

I THINK, dear God, the nicest prayer
Is thinking of You, everywhere!
All day long my heart keeps saying
"For You, God!" And that is praying.
So, out of all I think and do
I can make presents, God, for You.
O! I will always try to give
You lots of presents while I live!

—*Mary Dixon Thayer*

Gifts

The shepherds brought a little lamb
  To lie beside Him there,
The shepherds brought their softest wool,
  Do we bring nothing fair?

The Wise Men brought Him gold and myrrh
  And frankincense so sweet
But only the rich can hope to lay
  Such treasures at His feet.

Poor, yet we can bring Him one gift
  Who comes from Heaven above,
Better than lamb or gold or myrrh,
  And that is love.

—Julia Davis

The Toy Train

The children in the second-grade room of Saint Mary's School were filling a box to send to some poor children.

Their mothers had filled boxes with clothing, but the children were putting books and toys into this box.

Some of the books were beautiful. Sister had said: "Please do not put anything you do not want in the box. Bring something that you would like to keep. Bring the toy which you like best of all your toys."

John and Joseph told mother about the box. She said: "Do just what Sister told you to do. Put the toy which you like best in the box."

"I shall take my football for the box," said John.

Mother smiled. John's Christmas toys were all

broken or lost. The football was the only toy he had left.

"What shall you take, Joseph?" asked mother. Joseph took very good care of his toys. He had a great many toys, but everybody knew that he liked his toy train best of all.

"I think that I shall take my blocks," said Joseph.

"Very well," said his mother. But she did not smile when she said it.

So John took his football and Joseph took the blocks. But at noon Joseph brought the blocks home.

"I think that I shall keep these," he said. "I shall give away my Picture Puzzle Game."

So he took the picture puzzle to school. But that night he brought it home. "I did not put it in the box," he said. "I shall give away my train."

Mother had looked at Joseph very sadly when he brought home the game, but now she smiled.

"I am glad that you are giving the best toy that you have," she said.

On Friday morning Joseph took his train to school. The box was to be sent away on Saturday.

"The box for the poor children is full now. My train filled it up to the top," Joseph told his mother at noon.

Mother said, "Isn't that fine?"

After school John went home, but Joseph stayed to help Sister. She was called to the convent before the work was finished, so she said: "Do not wait for me, Joseph. Go home when the work is done. Thank you for helping me. Good night."

"Good night, Sister," said Joseph.

At last all the work was finished and Joseph was ready to go home.

Joseph stood at the door of the room. The box of toys was ready to be nailed. On Monday it would be gone. His train would be gone, too.

Joseph went over to the box and took out his train. "I want it for myself," he said. Then he went home.

Mother was at the window when Joseph came home. She saw him coming in, so she called to him.

"What have you there, dear?" she asked.

"I took back my train," said Joseph. "I want it for myself."

Mother said, "Joseph, come here!"

Joseph walked slowly over to mother. He felt very queer.

"Joseph," said his mother, "did you put your train in the box for the poor children?"

"Yes, mother," answered Joseph.

"Then it is not your train now. It belongs to the poor children. Take it back to school and put it in the box," said mother.

Joseph cried a little.

"May I put my new book in the box and keep the train?" he asked.

" No, dear," said his mother. "You know the train is the toy that you like best."

So Joseph went back to school. A man was in the second-grade room. He was putting the cover on the box.

"Here is something that belongs in the box," said Joseph.

He gave the train to the man and watched him put it into the box.

"You were just in time," said the man. "The box is full now."

Then he nailed the cover down.

On the way home Joseph went into the church for a few minutes. It was dark and still. The tabernacle door was shining in the dim light.

Joseph was glad now that the train was in the box. He was glad that he had given the best toy he had. He knew that Our Lord was glad, too. And it was a fine train.

The King's Highway

I saw her walking through the field,
   God's mother with her Son,
And every little flower-bell pealed
   To praise the Holy One.

Oh, every little rose upturned
   To wave as He did pass,
And every little sunbeam burned
   Its incense on the grass!

Oh, every little piping bird
   Did trumpet from the tree,
And every little lambkin heard,
   And danced, God's Lamb to see!

Oh, Nature all did serenade
   God's mother and her Son;
And then I knew why God had made
   His creatures—every one!

—*Rev. Hugh F. Blunt*

Mary, Mother of God

Mary, Mother of God,
  Of all God's creatures fairest,
Mary, Mother of God,
  Of earth the flower rarest.
Save Thy children, we pray,
Guide us, lest far away,
From Thee, Lady, we stray,
Mary, Mother of God.

Mary, Mother of God,
  In all our trials defend us,
Mary, Mother of God,
  We pray Thee, Queen befriend us.
By His Blood's saving stream,
Christ our souls did redeem,
Let Heaven's light on us beam,
Mary, Mother of God.

Mary, Mother of God,
  When death on us comes stealing,
Mary, Mother of God,
  Help us by Thy appealing.
With Christ for us then plead,
For us then intercede,
Thy prayer Jesus will heed,
Mary, Mother of God.

—from The Little Catholic's Choral

Christ among the Doctors by Heinrich Hoffman

The Boyhood of Jesus

When St. Joseph, the Blessed Virgin, and the Infant Savior came back from Egypt, they did not return to Bethlehem.

They went to live at Nazareth.

St. Joseph, you know, was a carpenter; and the Child Jesus helped him in his workshop.

The little Jesus was a very good Boy.

Everyone loved Him, because He was so kind and so good to all.

He never said an unkind word; He never did an unkind act.

His Blessed Mother taught Him to say His prayers as well as to read and to write.

When Jesus was twelve years of age, St. Joseph and the Blessed Virgin took Him to Jerusalem.

They went there to take part in a great feast.

At that time, there were neither trains nor electric cars.

So the Blessed Virgin, St. Joseph, and the Child Jesus walked with the other people from Nazareth to Jerusalem.

After staying in Jerusalem for a few days, they started for their home in Nazareth.

On their way back, the Blessed Virgin and St. Joseph missed the Boy Jesus. So they returned to Jerusalem, and looked everywhere for Him.

After some time they found Him in the temple, talking with the priests and asking them questions.

Jesus then returned to His home in Nazareth.

There He stayed until He was about thirty years of age.

Then He began to preach the Word of God to the people.

The Christ Child

The Christ-Child stood at Mary's knee,
 His hair was like a crown,
And all the flowers looked up at Him,
 And all the stars looked down.

—*G. K. Chesterton*

A Mother's Quest

"And not finding Him, they returned into Jerusalem seeking Him." (Luke 2:45)

Have you seen my little Love
   Going by your door?
Off He flew, my little Dove,
   And my heart is sore.

You would know my little Boy,
   Dressed in white and brown.
How my heart o'erflowed with joy
   As I wove His gown!

You would know Him from His hair,
   All of raven hue;
You would know Him anywhere,
   Once He looked at you.

Oh, if you should see my Own,
   Seeking out His home,
Tell Him how my joy has flown
   As the streets I roam.

Lead Him in beside thy hearth,
   Bid Him there remain;
Tell Him, though I search the earth,
   I will come again.

The Two Trinities (detail) by Bartolomé Esteban Murillo

And if hungry He should be,
   Give Him of your bread;
If He nods so wearily,
   Make His little bed.

Woman, if you see my Boy,
   Oh, to Him be kind!
You will have the fullest joy, —
   Lo, 'tis God you'll find!

—*Rev. Hugh F. Blunt*

The Annunciation by H.J. Sinkel

The Annunciation

Last autumn, four of my friends were sitting with me by the fireside. We were talking about vacation.

When we had finished, Mary asked: "Who is the most beautiful woman that ever lived?"

After a great many answers were given, Margaret said: "I think the Blessed Virgin Mary is the most beautiful woman that ever lived."

"I think you are right," said Rose.

Just then Mrs. Shine came into the room.

"Mother," said Helen, "please tell us about the Blessed Virgin Mary."

Mrs. Shine told this story:

"One day when the Blessed Virgin Mary was alone in her room, an angel stood beside her.

"When the Blessed Virgin Mary saw the angel, she was afraid.

"'Do not be afraid,' said he, 'God has sent me to you with a message.'

"'A message from God for me! What can it be?'

"'He told me to tell you that He is going to send you a little Son, and you must call Him "Jesus."'

"'Since God wants it, I am willing,' said the Blessed Virgin.

"The angel's visit made the Blessed Virgin very happy.

"God wanted her to be the mother of the Infant Jesus.

"God loved her because she was so good."

The Baptism of Jesus

Unto St. John the Baptist,
   Who preached, baptizing men,
Came Christ, and on His sacred head
   Was poured the water then.
And when 'twas done, the heavens oped,
   And God spoke from the skies:
"See! This is My beloved Son
   Whom I so dearly prize!"

The Children of the King

Once upon a time, a little boy and a little girl lived in a great castle. Their father was a king and he ruled the country for many miles around.

In the gardens of the castle there was everything that could make a boy or girl happy.

There were beautiful flowers, and every child could pick as many of them as he liked. There were thick bushes that made the best place in the world for hide-and-seek and a great hollow tree that made the jolliest kind of a make-believe house. There was even a lake where the boys sailed their boats and the girls waded.

No wonder all the children who lived near the castle liked to come there to play.

One day ugly sounds came from the beautiful garden. Angry voices reached the king in his throne room. In a moment the door of the throne room flew open and the little prince and princess came running to their father. Their cross faces showed plainly that they had been quarreling.

They told their father what had happened. He looked at them kindly but sadly. "My children," he said, "it is not right for any child to quarrel, but for you to quarrel is very wrong indeed, for you are the children of a king."

On the day that we were baptized we were made children of God, the King of Kings. We should always remember the honor that is ours. We must try never to do anything that is unworthy of our Father. Like the father of the prince and princess, God wishes us always to remember that we are the children of a King.

Speak Little Voice

Speak, little voice within me, speak!
    Set is my heart to hear;
Low is the light and the night is bleak,
    Tell me that God is near.

Speak, little voice, and strongly say
    I am His little child;
Counsel and lead me along the way,—
    Life is a pathway wild.

God is my Father,—O little voice,
    This do you whisper me;
Father all-watchful, so I rejoice,
    Bleak though the night may be.

—Rev. Michael Earls, S. J.

The Old Woman and the Cakes

Once a little old woman was baking cakes. She was wearing a black dress and a small white apron. On her head was a red cap.

A poor old man came to her kitchen door and said, "I am hungry, good woman. Please give me one of your cakes."

The old woman said, "These cakes are too large to give away. I will bake you a little cake. That will be plenty for you."

So she made a very small cake. She rolled it and rolled it. Then she patted it and patted it, and put it into the oven.

But the cake began to grow bigger and bigger.

"I will keep this cake," said the old woman. "It is too big to give away." So she kept the cake for herself.

Then she made a tiny little cake. She rolled it and rolled it and patted it and patted it until it was very flat.

"This will be large enough for you," she said, as she put it into the oven.

But it began to grow bigger, too.

"I will not give you this cake," said the old woman. "I want it myself. It is much too big for a fellow like you."

So she kept that cake for herself.

She tried again. This time she made a tiny flat cake as small as a bean.

But that cake began to grow, too. It grew bigger and bigger and bigger.

"I will not give you a cake at all," said the old woman. "These cakes are too big to give away. I want to eat them myself."

So the poor old man went away hungry.

The old woman swept her kitchen and sat down alone to eat the cakes.

Now comes the strangest part of this story.

As the old woman was eating, she began to grow smaller and smaller.

Her nose became a sharp bill. She looked at her arms and saw that they had been changed to black wings. And her feet were sharp claws.

She was still wearing the black dress and white apron and red cap. But they were all feathers!

She had been changed into a bird.

Perhaps you will see this little old woman some day. She hops up and down trees, hunting for bugs and worms.

You will know her when you see her. You will say, "There is the black dress and the little white apron that she was wearing in her kitchen. On her head is the red cap, too."

For people say that the old woman who would not give away even one tiny cake was changed into a woodpecker.

An Honest Boy

Fred Green, the oldest of six children, was looking for work one day.

While walking down Summer Street, he saw a gentleman drop some money.

Fred picked it up, ran after the gentleman, and said to him: "You dropped this money, sir."

"You must be mistaken, my boy."

"Oh, no, sir," said Fred; "I saw the money drop from your hand when you paid the hackman."

"Why, that was a few streets back," said the gentleman. "Has your mother much money, my good boy?"

"She has very little, sir. That is why I am looking for work. My father is dead, and I am the oldest of six children."

"Why did you not keep the money you found?" said the gentleman.

"Because that money is yours, sir, and not mine. I should like to earn some money, but I will not steal it."

Then the gentleman thanked Fred, and asked him where he lived.

A few weeks later, he called at Fred's house, and told him that he had work for him in a bank.

"I am very thankful to you, sir," said Fred. "You are very kind."

"You need not thank me, Fred. You are just the kind of a boy that I have been looking for.

"You are honest; you are manly; you are thoughtful; and you are willing to work to help your mother."

The Temptation of Christ by Ary Scheffer

The Temptation of Jesus

Then forth into the desert drear
   Our blessed Lord was led.
And there He stayed, and fasted long,
   Till forty days had sped.
But when the devil, tempting, came,
   Our Saviour cried: "Begone!
The Lord thy God shalt thou adore:
   And serve but Him alone!"

St. Peter's Answer

"Whom say ye that I am?" He asked.
    St. Peter raised his head:
"Thou art the Christ, the Son of God,
    The living God!" he said.
And then Our Savior, answering
    Said, "Peter, thou art blest;
Upon thee will I build My Church;
    Upon thee shall it rest."

The Delivery of the Keys to Saint Peter by Pietro Perugino

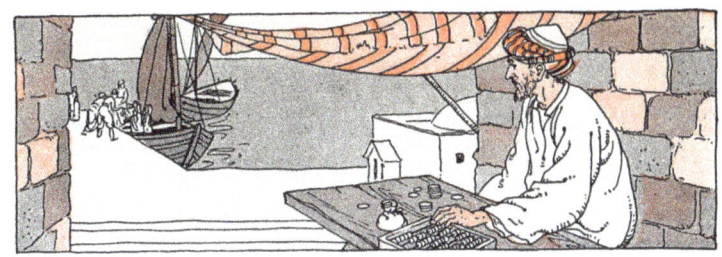

The Calling of Saint Matthew

Saint Matthew was sitting in his little toll-house. It was a sunny afternoon. Saint Matthew was watching the little boats on the blue water, but he was thinking about Our Lord.

A boat was coming to land. It came nearer and nearer. Jesus was in the boat. It stopped at the landing place, and Our Lord and His friends got out.

They stopped at the toll-house. Then they passed down the street. Matthew watched them go. He wanted to go, too.

Soon Matthew saw Our Lord and His friends coming back. He stood at the door of his little house.

Would Jesus look at him? Matthew was afraid that He would pass by and not see him.

Our Lord came nearer and nearer. He was at the door! Matthew watched and watched, but Jesus passed by.

But when He had gone a little way, He turned and looked at Matthew.

"Follow Me," He said.

And Matthew went with Him.

Mother Dear, Pray for Me

The Lord's First Miracle

Of our dear Lord's first miracle
  We read, in Holy Text:
How at the feast the wine had failed
  And all were shamed and vext.
His Mother's pleading words He heard,
  And changed, so all could see:
The brimming water into wine,
  At Cana of Galilee!

Finding You

DEAR God, I wish I could have been
  Among those girls and boys
You called to come and talk to You,
  And who left all their toys,
And ran and climbed up on Your knee,
  And held Your hand, and sat
Around You, learning lovely things—
  I *wish* I had done that!

But God, I know that even now
   I can get close to You.
I know You still love children—yes
   Indeed! I know You do!
And so I often slip away
   Into the Church, and kneel
Down at the altar where You are,
   And tell You all I feel.
I cannot see Your face, and yet
   I know that You are there.
I know I'm just as close to You
   As all those children were!

—*Mary Dixon Thayer*

The Helper

My crown of thorns is great and strong,
My scourging cords are thick and long,
My cross is monstrous high and wide;
What matter? God is at my side.

—Rev. Hugh F. Blunt

A Bunch of Golden Keys

A bunch of golden keys is mine
  To make each day with gladness shine.

"Good morning!" that's the golden key
  That unlocks every door for me.

When evening comes, "Good night!" I say,
  And close the door of each glad day.

When at the table "If you please"
  I take from off my bunch of keys.

When friends give anything to me,
  I'll use the little "Thank you" key.

"Excuse me," "Beg your pardon," too,
  When by mistake some harm I do.

Or if unkindly harm I've given,
   With "Forgive me" key I'll be forgiven.

On a golden ring these keys I'll bind,
   This is its motto: "Be ye kind."

I'll often use each golden key,
   And so a happy child I'll be.

Little Things

Hearts good and true
   Have wishes few,
In narrow circles bounded;
   And hope that lives
   On what God gives,
Is Christian hope well founded.

Small things are best—
   Grief and unrest
With wealth and rank are given;
   But little things
   On little wings
Bear little souls to heaven.

—Father Frederick William Faber

What Have I?

The Shepherds had an Angel,
   The Wise Men had a Star,
But what have I, a little child,
   To guide me home from far,
Where glad stars sing together
   And singing angels are?

—*Christina Rossetti*

Our Lord Cures the Lame Man

Near Jerusalem there was a pond of water. It was a wonderful pond.

Once a year God sent an angel to the pond. The angel moved the water.

The first sick person going into the water after the angel had moved it was made well.

Many sick persons stayed near the pond. They stayed there day after day. They waited for the angel to move the water. They wished to be made well.

One day our Lord was going to Jerusalem. He passed by the wonderful pond.

There He saw a poor lame man. The man had been lame a long time. He could not walk alone.

"My son," said our dear Lord, "how long have you been here?"

"I have been here thirty-eight years, good Master," said the lame man.

"Do you wish to be made well?" asked our Lord.

"Yes, good Master," said the poor lame man. "I wish to be made well. For thirty-eight years I have waited. Each year God sends an angel to the pond. The angel moves the waters.

"Then I try to go to the pond. But I am very slow. I am so lame that I cannot walk. I have no one to help me. So another sick person goes into the pond before me. Then I must wait another year.

"But God is good. I know He will cure me some time."

Our dear Lord was sorry for the poor lame man. He put His hand on the lame man's head.

Then He blessed him and said, "Arise, My son, take up your bed, and walk."

The lame man arose. He took up his bed. He walked around the pond.

How happy he was!

He had been lame for thirty-eight years. Our dear Lord had cured him. Now he could go to his home.

He wished to thank our Lord, but He had walked away.

That day the man met our Lord again.

"Thank You, kind Master," he said. "Thank You for making me well."

"I have made you well, My son," said our Lord, "because I wish you to love God. I wish you to be good always."

Then our Lord went away.

The well-known hymn on the next page was originally a German hymn based on the Latin *Te Deum,* written in 1744 by an Austrian priest. In 1858 it was then translated into English by Father Clarence Augustus Walworth. This is his original version.

Holy God, We Praise Thy Name

1. Holy God, we praise Thy name;
   Lord of all, we bow before Thee.
   All on earth Thy scepter claim;
   All in heav'n above adore Thee.
   Infinite Thy vast domain;
   Everlasting is Thy reign.

2. Hark, the glad celestial hymn
   Angel choirs above are raising;
   Cherubim and Seraphim,
   In unceasing chorus praising,
   Fill the heav'ns with sweet accord:
   "Holy, holy, holy Lord!"

3. Lo, the apostolic train
   Joins Thy sacred name to hallow;
   Prophets swell the glad refrain,
   And the white-robed martyrs follow.
   And from morn to set of sun,
   Through the church the song goes on.

4. Holy Father, Holy Son,
   Holy Spirit, three we name Thee,
   Though in essence only One;
   Undivided God, we claim Thee,
   And, adoring, bend the knee
   While we own the mystery.

The Making of Birds

God made Him birds in a pleasant humor;
   Tired of planets and suns was He.
He said, "I will add a glory to summer,
   Gifts for my creatures banished from Me!"

He had a thought and it set Him smiling,
   Of the shape of a bird and its glancing head,
Its dainty air and its grace beguiling:
   "I will make feathers," the Lord God said.

He made the robin: He made the swallow;
   His deft hands moulding the shape to His mood;

The thrush, the lark, and the finch to follow,
And laughed to see that His work was good.

He who has given men gift of laughter,
  Made in His image; He fashioned fit
The blink of the owl and the stork thereafter,
  The little wren and the long-tailed tit.

He spent in the making His wit and fancies;
  The wing-feathers He fashioned them strong;
Deft and dear as daisies and pansies,
  He crowned His work with the gift of song.

"Dearlings," He said, "make songs for my praises!"
  He tossed them loose to the sun and wind,
Airily sweet as pansies and daisies;
  He taught them to build a nest to their mind.

The dear Lord God of His glories weary—
  Christ our Lord had the heart of a boy—
Made Him birds in a moment merry,
  Bade them soar and sing for his joy.

                      —*Katharine Tynan Hinkson*

The Rich Ruler's Daughter

A very rich ruler was living in Jerusalem at the time when Jesus was there. This ruler's name was Jairus. Jairus had a beautiful little daughter whom he loved very much.

One day this little girl became ill. Each day she grew worse and worse. At last she was so ill that her father was afraid she was not going to get well.

The poor father did not know what to do. Then he remembered that one of the servants had told him of a holy Man, named Jesus. This Man had cured many sick people. He had made the blind to see. He had made the lame to walk and the deaf to hear. He had even raised the dead to life.

"I will go to Jesus," he said. "I will ask Him to cure my daughter."

Jairus went to the temple. There he saw a number of people gathered together. As he came closer he saw a Man talking to the people. "This must be Jesus," he said to himself.

Jairus went to Jesus. He said, "Lord, my daughter is very sick. Come to my house. Lay Your hand upon her head so that she may get well."

Our Lord felt sorry for Jairus. "I will come to see your daughter," He said.

A short way from the house a servant met Jairus. He said, "Your daughter has just died." The father wept. "Do not weep. Your daughter is not dead; she is sleeping," Our Lord said.

They walked on until they reached the house. The people there were crying.

Our Lord went into the room where the little girl was lying. He said, "The girl is not dead. She is sleeping."

Jesus took hold of her hand. Then He said, "Arise."

The little girl opened her eyes at once. She saw the beautiful face of Jesus. Then she arose from her bed and stood before her happy father, well and strong.

Raising the Son of the Widow of Naim by Heinrich Hofmann

The Kindness of Jesus

During the three years that Jesus preached to the people, He did many very wonderful things.

One day, as He was walking along the street, He met a funeral.

The only son of a poor woman was being carried to the grave.

The mother was crying as if her heart would break.

Our Blessed Lord stopped the funeral, and said to the mother: "Weep not."

Then He said to him who was dead: "Young man, I say to thee, arise."

And, wonderful to relate, he that was dead, sat up and began to speak.

When the people saw what Jesus had done, they fell on their knees, and gave thanks to God.

The poor mother's heart was now filled with joy. She did not forget to thank our dear Lord.

See how very kind and good Jesus was to that sad mother!

The Daughter of Jairus

One day, a certain ruler came
  And worshiping, he said:
"In yonder house, my only child,
  My daughter, lieth dead.
Yet shall she live if Thou but say
  The word, and take her hand!"
Our Saviour called the little maid:
  Who lived at His command!

The Poor Widow's Son

Again, outside the city gates
  Of Naim, a mother old,
A widow, walked beside the bier,
  Where lifeless lay, and cold,
The body of her only child.
  Our Saviour, tenderly
Said, "Mother, weep not! See, I give
  Thy living son to thee!"

Night and Day

When I run about all day,
When I kneel at night to pray,
    God sees.

When I'm dreaming in the dark,
When I lie awake and hark,
    God sees.

Need I ever know a fear?
Night and day my Father's near.
    God sees.

—*Mary Mapes Dodge*

The Storm

It was evening. The day had been warm. Jesus said to His disciples, "Let us go out on the water."

So they got into a boat and went out on the Sea of Galilee.

Jesus was tired. Great crowds had followed Him all day. He had preached to them and had cured many who were sick.

After Jesus got into the boat He lay down. Soon He was fast asleep. For a while, the wind blew the boat gently across the waters.

Suddenly a dark cloud came into the sky. A strong wind swept over the sea. Big waves dashed against the side of the boat. The boat rocked up and down. Water came into the boat. Then it began to sink.

The disciples who were in the boat were afraid. They went over to where Jesus was sleeping. They woke Him.

"Lord, save us!" they said.

Jesus said to them, "Why are you afraid? O you of little faith!"

Jesus arose and said to the sea, "Peace, be still."

The waves fell. The wind was still.

The disciples wondered. They said, "Who is This That commands the winds and the sea, and they obey Him?"

Saint Valentine

Many of you may want to know how we came to have Saint Valentine's Day. This story tells why we send valentines.

Long ago there lived in Rome a man named Valentine. He was an old man who lived in a large house with a beautiful garden. Valentine loved children and was always kind to them. There were children always playing in his garden. Many times he came out to watch them. Sometimes he told them stories about Jesus.

Valentine was also very good to the poor people. When they had no food to eat, he would leave food at their doors.

One day the children found the garden closed. The king had put Valentine in prison because he had told the people about Christ.

The story is told that while Valentine was in prison he wanted to tell his friends that he remembered them and loved them. He could not send them food, but he could send them letters of love and faith. So he wrote letters to all his friends

and to the children who played in his garden.

Long, long after Valentine died, the people still remembered how good he had been. They called him Saint Valentine. They did not forget how he sent letters of love to all his friends while he was in prison.

Now we remember Saint Valentine on the fourteenth of February by sending letters of love to our friends.

The Good Shepherd
by Bernhard Plockhorst

Jesus, Tender Shepherd

Mary (Lundie) Duncan, 1839   John Stainer, 1898

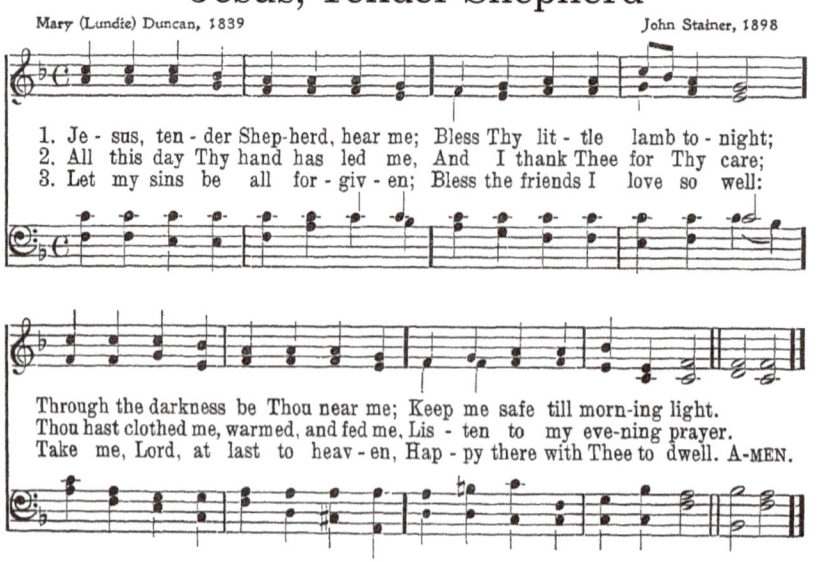

1. Je - sus, ten - der Shep-herd, hear me; Bless Thy lit - tle lamb to - night;
2. All this day Thy hand has led me, And I thank Thee for Thy care;
3. Let my sins be all for - giv - en; Bless the friends I love so well:

Through the darkness be Thou near me; Keep me safe till morn-ing light.
Thou hast clothed me, warmed, and fed me, Lis - ten to my eve-ning prayer.
Take me, Lord, at last to heav - en, Hap - py there with Thee to dwell. A-MEN.

Sheep and Lambs

All in the April evening,
  April airs were abroad;
The sheep with their little lambs
  Passed me by on the road.

The sheep with their little lambs
  Passed me by on the road;
All in the April evening
  I thought on the Lamb of God.

The lambs were weary and crying
  With a weak, human cry.
I thought on the Lamb of God
  Going meekly to die.

Up in the blue, blue mountains
  Dewy pastures are sweet;
Rest for the little bodies,
  Rest for the little feet.

But for the Lamb of God,
  Up on the hill-top green,
Only a Cross of shame
  Two stark crosses between.

All in the April evening,
  April airs were abroad;
I saw the sheep with their lambs,
  And thought on the Lamb of God.

—Katharine Tynan Hinkson

The Shepherdess

SHE walks—the lady of my delight—
   A shepherdess of sheep.
Her flocks are thoughts. She keeps them white;
   She guards them from the steep;
She feeds them on the fragrant height,
   And folds them in for sleep.

She roams maternal hills and bright,
   Dark valleys safe and deep.
Into that tender breast at night
   The chastest stars may peep.
She walks—the lady of my delight—
   A shepherdess of sheep.

She holds her little thoughts in sight,
   Though gay they run and leap.
She is so circumspect and right;
   She has her soul to keep.
She walks—the lady of my delight—
   A shepherdess of sheep.

—Alice Meynell

The Shepherdess by Johann Hofner

The Divine Shepherd by Bartolomé Esteban Murillo

I Will Follow Thee

I would be Thy little lamb,
   I would follow Thee,
Tender Shepherd! In Thine arms,
   I would carried be.

Do Thou lead me all the day
   In the safe and narrow way,
Never, never let me stray
   Dearest Lord! from Thee.

Glad I lisp my simple prayers,
   Knowing Thou art near;
When I ask Thy tender care
   Thou dost love to hear.

Softly in my heart I know
   'Tis Thy voice that murmurs low—
"Dearest child! I love thee so
   That I died for thee."

Thou didst lay Thy glory by,
   O my Saviour dear!
In a manger Thou didst lie,
   Cold, and hard, and drear.

At Thy gentle Mother's side,
   Let me too with Thee abide,
Dear St. Joseph was Thy guide
   In Thy work or play.

In that holy family
   Let me numbered be;
Meditating day by day
   On that wondrous Three.

Then, when I am older grown,
   Thou wilt be my very own,
Coming from Thine altar-throne
   To dwell awhile with me.

In Thy footsteps day by day,
   Jesus! Keep Thou me;
From Thy side I'll never stray,
   I will follow Thee.

The Lamb

Little Lamb who made thee
  Dost thou know who made thee,
Gave thee life and bid thee feed
By the stream and o'er the mead;
Gave thee clothing of delight,
Softest clothing wooly bright;
Gave thee such a tender voice,
Making all the vales rejoice?
    Little Lamb who made thee?
    Dost thou know who made thee?

    Little Lamb I'll tell thee;
    Little Lamb I'll tell thee:
He is callèd by thy name,
For he calls himself a Lamb.
He is meek and he is mild,
He became a little child.
I a child, and thou a lamb,
We are callèd by his name.
    Little Lamb God bless thee!
    Little Lamb God bless thee!

—*William Blake*

The Good Shepherd

Our Lord is the Good Shepherd.
  His little lamb am I,
And to His Arms I'll quickly run
  When there is danger nigh.

How safe I am with Jesus!
  What care He takes of me!
A very loving little lamb
  I always ought to be.

The Good Shepherd

In the land where Jesus lived when He was on earth, there were many sheep. These sheep were taken to the pasture in the daytime. The night they spent in the sheepfold. A sheepfold is a place around which is a wall to keep out wild animals.

In the morning the door of the sheepfold was opened. The shepherd stood at the door and called his flock. His sheep came at his call. He let them out of the fold and counted them as they passed through the door. Then he led them to the pasture, where they ate the tender green grass. When there was no more grass for the sheep in one pasture, the shepherd led them to a new one. He was always careful that his sheep had plenty of food.

The shepherd watched his flock all day. The little lambs played and frisked about. If any of the sheep or lambs strayed away from the others, the shepherd called them back.

In the evening the shepherd led his flock back to the fold. Some of the little lambs would get very tired on the way back, because they had played all day. Then they could not walk as fast as the big sheep.

Whenever the shepherd saw one of these tired little lambs, he picked it up. Sometimes he carried it on his shoulders. If it were a cold evening he carried it under his warm cloak.

When the sheep came to the fold, they were put into it for the night. The shepherd stayed with them to protect them. Sometimes wild animals leaped into the fold. The shepherd tried hard to drive them out. He was not always able to do this, for some of the animals were very strong. Many times they hurt the shepherd. Sometimes they even killed him.

One day Jesus was talking to the people, as He often did. He wanted them to understand how great His love is. These people knew how well the shepherds took care of their flocks. So Jesus said to the people, "I am the good shepherd. The good shepherd gives his life for his sheep."

We know what a good shepherd Jesus is. He is always watching over us. He gave His life for us when He died on the cross. He feeds us with His own Body and Blood in Holy Communion.

> Loving Shepherd, Thou didst give
>   Thine own life that I might live;
> May I love Thee day by day,
>   Gladly Thy sweet will obey.
>
> Where Thou leadest may I go,
>   Walking in Thy steps below;
> Then before Thy Father's throne,
>   Jesus, claim me for Thine own.

My Neighbor

My neighbor as myself to love,
　Thou hast commanded me,
And in obedience I prove
　That Thou Thyself art he.

　　　　　—Rev. John Banister Tabb

A Useful Lesson

Prayers and good works
　　　within your memory store
And at stray moments,
　　　say them o'er and o'er;
'Twill help to hallow
　　　all your work and play.
And holy thoughts
　　　will keep bad thoughts away.

　　　　　—Rev. M. Russell, S.J.

The Lowest Place

Give me the lowest place; not that I dare
   Ask for that lowest place, but Thou hast died
That I might live and share
   Thy glory by Thy side.

Give me the lowest place; or if for me
   That lowest place too high, make one more low
Where I may sit and see
   My God and love Thee so.

—Christina Rossetti

Come to Jesus

SOULS of men! why will ye scatter
  Like a crowd of frightened sheep?
Foolish hearts! why will ye wander
  From a love so true and deep?

Was there ever kindest shepherd
  Half so gentle, half so sweet,
As the Saviour who would have us
  Come and gather round His Feet?

It is God: His love looks mighty,
  But is mightier than it seems:
'Tis our Father: and His fondness
  Goes far out beyond our dreams.

There s a wideness in God's mercy,
  Like the wideness of the sea:
There' s a kindness in His justice,
  Which is more than liberty.

There is no place where earth's sorrows
  Are more felt than up in Heaven;
There is no place where earth's failings
  Have such kindly judgment given.

There is welcome for the sinner,
  And more graces for the good;
There is mercy with the Saviour;
  There is healing in His Blood.

There is grace enough for thousands
  Of new worlds as great as this;
There is room for fresh creations
  In that upper home of bliss.

For the love of God is broader
  Than the measures of man's mind;
And the Heart of the Eternal
  Is most wonderfully kind.

But we make His love too narrow
  By false limits of our own;
And we magnify His strictness
  With a zeal He will not own.

There is plentiful redemption
  In the Blood that has been shed;
There is joy for all the members
  In the sorrows of the Head.

'Tis not all we owe to Jesus;
  It is something more than all;
Greater good because of evil,
  Larger mercy through the fall.

Pining Souls! come nearer Jesus,
  And oh come not doubting thus,
But with faith that trusts more bravely
  His huge tenderness for us.

If our love were but more simple,
  We should take Him at His word;
And our lives would be all sunshine
  In the sweetness of our Lord.

—*Father Frederick William Faber*

Discontent

Down in a field, one day in June,
    The flowers all bloomed together,
Save one, who tried to hide herself,
    And drooped that pleasant weather.

A robin who had soared too high,
    And felt a little lazy,
Was resting near a buttercup,
    Who wished she were a daisy.

For daisies grow so trim and tall!
    She always had a passion
For wearing frills about her neck,
    In just the daisies' fashion.

And buttercups must always be
    The same old tiresome color,

While daisies dress in gold and white,
   Although their gold is duller.

"Dear robin," said this sad young flower,
   "Perhaps you'd not mind trying
To find a nice white frill for me,
   Some day, when you are flying?"

"You silly thing!" the robin said;
   "I think you must be crazy!
I'd rather be my honest self
   Than any made-up daisy.

"You're nicer in your own bright gown,
   The little children love you;
Be the best buttercup you can,
   And think no flower above you.

"Though swallows leave me out of sight,
   We'd better keep our places;
Perhaps the world would all go wrong
   With one too many daisies.

"Look bravely up into the sky,
   And be content with knowing
That God wished for a buttercup
   Just here, where you are growing."

—*Sarah Orne Jewett*

The Very Time

I USED to think, if I'd been bad,
I'd better stay away
From You, dear God, I used to think
I might as well not pray.
I used to think, if I'd been bad,
You wouldn't want me to—
And so I didn't pray, but now
Of course I always do.
Now when I have been bad, dear God,
I always quickly fall
Down on my knees for then—O! then
I need you most of all!

—*Mary Dixon Thayer*

The Prodigal Son

The sun was shining when the prodigal son went away. He was very happy. His purse was full of money. He had said good-by to his father and brother. It was fun to be going away from home.

He had never felt so gay.

He stopped in a far country. He had never seen so beautiful a place. He forgot his father and his home. Everybody liked the young man because he was so rich and gay. They helped him to spend his money. It did not take very long.

Then hard times came. The prodigal son wanted to go to work, but no one had work to give him. He was hungry and tired now, and he was very, very sad.

At last he did get work, but it was not very pleasant. He took care of pigs. Sometimes he was so hungry that he wanted to eat the food that was for the pigs.

One day he said to himself: "I am going back to my father's house. He is kind to everyone. He will give me work and food."

So he set out for home.

It was a long, hard way from the far country. The prodigal son had no money now. He was hungry and tired, too, but he went on and on and on. At last he came to his father's house. He had forgotten how beautiful it was!

He did not have time to ask his father to forgive him. His father ran to meet him, crying: "Welcome home, my son! My dear lost boy, welcome home!"

Everybody was glad that he had come home, and he was happy, too.

The Load of Wood

It was getting dark. The snow had been falling all day. Everything was covered with a beautiful white cloak.

The children of the convent school were at supper. Mother Gertrude sat at the head of the table. She smiled at her hungry little girls. She liked to hear them talk.

Just then Sister Damian came to her. She looked frightened.

"Mother," she said, "we have only a few sticks of wood."

"I asked Mr. Field to send a load of wood today. Didn't it come?" asked Mother Gertrude.

"No, Mother," said Sister Damian. "There are only a few sticks in the shed. It is going to be a cold night, too."

"Let us have night prayers now. We will ask Saint Joseph to send some wood. Then the children can go to bed," said Mother Gertrude.

So after supper everybody went to the chapel. They said the rosary and the night prayers. They asked Saint Joseph to take care of them.

Mother Gertrude said, "Saint Joseph, please send us some wood tonight!"

The children went to bed. They were soon fast asleep. The house was getting very cold.

Sister Damian said, "O Mother! What are we going to do tomorrow?"

Mother Gertrude smiled.

"Saint Joseph will take care of us," she said.

There was a rap at the door and Mother Gertrude and Sister Damian answered it. A man in a big fur coat stood at the door.

"Here is your load of wood, Sisters," he said. "Shall I put it in the shed?"

"Yes, thank you," said Mother. "We are glad to get the wood tonight."

When the wood was put away in the shed the man said: "Good night, Sisters! God bless you!" Then he went away.

The next day was sunny. It was warmer too. So

Mother Gertrude and Sister Damian went to pay for the wood.

But Mr. Field said: "I sent you no wood last night. We were getting it ready to send when you came in."

The Sisters asked everybody about the wood. No one had sent it to them. No one knew the man in the big fur coat.

Mr. Field came to the convent to look at the wood.

"This must have come from far away. It does not grow near here," he said.

That night Sister Damian said to Mother Gertrude, "Mother, did Saint Joseph bring that load of wood?"

Mother smiled. "I do not know who brought it," she said, "but I do know that Saint Joseph sent it."

A Child's Evening Prayer

Ere on my bed my limbs I lay,
  God grant me grace my prayers to say:
O God! preserve my mother dear
  In strength and health for many a year;
And, O! preserve my father too,
  And may I pay him reverence due;
And may I my best thoughts employ
  To be my parents' hope and joy;
And, O! preserve my brothers both
  From evil doings and from sloth,
And may we always love each other,
  Our friends, our father, and our mother,
And still, O Lord, to me impart
  An innocent and grateful heart,
That after my last sleep I may
  Awake to thy eternal day! Amen.

—Samuel Taylor Coleridge

Different Ways

Dear God, I try to tell You
Through all the live-long day
"I love You!" And to say it
In every sort of way.
I say it in the morning
By jumping out of bed
Just when I ought to do it
You know, dear God, instead
Of lying there and thinking
How comfy beds can be—
For that would not be loving
You, God—but loving me!
And then I say "I love You!"
By washing as I should,
And all day long I say it
By trying to be good...
"I love You, God! I love You!"
There are as many ways
Of saying that I love You
As there are nights and days!

—*Mary Dixon Thayer*

A Prayer to Mary

Dear Mother, pray for me,
   That God's grace in me dwell;
Of Jesus ask this boon:
   That I may love Him well—

That I may love Him well;
   And, to Him ever true,
Through all this coming year
   No deed of mine may rue.

God's Mother, pray for me,
   This year and all my days;
So I may come to heaven,
   And thee and Jesus praise.

—*Rev. H.G. Hughes*

Thoughts

I WANT to think of You, dear God,
A million times a day—
At home, and when I am in school,
And when I am at play!
No matter who is by, nor where
I am, nor what I do,
I know that I can always send
A thought, dear God, to You!

—*Mary Dixon Thayer*

A Prayer

Mary! Dearest Mother!
　From thy heavenly height
Look on us, thy children,
　Lost in earth's dark night.

Daughter of the Father!
　Lady kind and sweet!
Lead us to our Father;
　Leave us at His feet.

Jesus! Hear Thy children
　From Thy throne above;
Give us love of Mary
　As Thou wouldst have us love.

The Lord's Prayer

One day Jesus went out on a lonely hill to pray.

The men who were with Jesus said, "Master, teach us to pray."

Then Jesus taught the men the prayer, *Our Father*.

It is called The Lord's Prayer.

We kneel to say it every day.

The Lord's Prayer is said everywhere.

Triumphal Hymn for Palm Sunday

All glory, laud and honor
To Thee, O Christ, we bring,
And sing like Sion's children,
Hosannas to Our King.

For Thou art king, Lord Jesus,
Of David's royal line,
And blest are all who serve Thee
And call Thy name divine.

The saints and holy angels
Exalt in heaven Thy name,
And men on earth forever
Thy glory shall proclaim.

As came the Jews to meet Thee
With palms upon the way.
So we with prayerful voices
Lift up our songs to-day.

As they loud praises paid Thee
Upon the road of pain,
So we with sounding music
Salute Thy endless reign.

As their devotion pleased Thee,
So be our offering—
The song, the prayer, the praises,
We bring Thee, gentle King.

—Translation by D. J. Donahoe.

Blessed Candle

Hallowed light,
Quivering in the night,
How pure thy gleam, how mild!
   Silent prayer,
On the altar, where
There rests an Infant Child!
   Silver flame,
Whispering the Name
Of Jesus, Infant Child!

—*Joseph Kinney Collins*

Communion

Mother Mary, thee I see
Bringing Him, thy Babe, to me,
Thou dost say, with trusting smile:
"Hold Him, dear, a little while."
Mother Mary, pity me,
For He struggles to be free!
My heart, my arms—He finds defiled:
I am unworthy of thy Child.
Mary, Mother, charity!
Bring thy Baby back to me!

—*Caroline Giltinian*

After a Visit to the Blessed Sacrament

Whenever in pain or sin,
  I love to enter in
Before some altar door,
  God's favor to implore.

We talk a little while—
  A word or two, a smile,
His love's absolving kiss,
  Such reverential bliss!

And then with clearer ken
  I face life's ways again;
'Mid all its deafening roar,
  King of my soul once more!

—*S.M. St. John*

A Child's Wish

I wish I were the little key
That locks Love's Captive in,
And lets Him out to go and free
A sinful heart from sin.

I wish I were the little bell
That tinkles for the Host,
When God comes down each day to dwell
With hearts He loves the most.

I wish I were the chalice fair,
That holds the Blood of Love,
When every flash lights holy prayer
Upon its way above.

I wish I were the little flower
So near the Host's sweet face,
Or like the light that half an hour
Burns on the shrine of grace.

I wish I were the altar where,
As on His mother's breast,
Christ nestles, like a child, fore'er
In Eucharistic rest.

But, oh! My God, I wish the most
That my poor heart may be
A home all holy for each Host
That comes in love to me.

—*Rev. Abram J. Ryan*

Blessed Imelda

This is the story of a little girl named Imelda, who lived many years ago. She loved Jesus very much. When she was nine years old, she went to live in a convent with the Sisters.

At the time Imelda lived, children did not receive Holy Communion until they were much older. Imelda was very sad and lonely because she could not receive Jesus in Holy Communion. When she saw the Sisters receiving Holy Communion, she would say, "O good Jesus, please come to me. You are so good and You know how much I want to receive You."

Imelda always tried to be good. She did without candy and many other things she liked. She was always kind to her friends. Imelda did all this because she wanted to show Jesus that she loved Him.

When she felt sad because she could not receive Jesus in Holy Communion, she tried to do still more to show Jesus how much she loved Him. She tried to say her prayers even better than before. She tried to be still more kind to her friends. She wanted to do without more things she liked, so that Jesus would answer her prayer.

One day, after Imelda had lived in the convent two years, she was in the chapel with the nuns. At the time for Holy Communion, all the Sisters went to receive Jesus. How Imelda wanted to receive Jesus too! She prayed and prayed to Jesus. "Dear Jesus," she said, "please come to me. I love You so much."

Then Jesus answered her prayer. After the Sisters left the chapel, Imelda stayed there alone. She was crying because she wanted Jesus to come to her. She was so lonely without Him.

Soon an odor of sweet flowers began to fill the whole convent. The Sisters were surprised.

They went to see where the odor was coming from. They went to the chapel. There they saw a bright ray of light. In the midst of it Imelda was kneeling in prayer. As the Sisters looked, a host left the Tabernacle, floated through the air, and stood over the little girl's head. Jesus was showing the Sisters that He wanted to give Himself to little Imelda.

The Sisters called the priest at once. He put on his vestments and went to the place where Imelda was kneeling. He placed a paten under the host. It

came down and rested upon the paten. Then the priest gave little Imelda her first Holy Communion.

How wonderful it was to have Jesus so near! Imelda was very happy. The Sisters again left the chapel. Imelda knelt and prayed.

After Imelda had been in the chapel a long time, one of the Sisters went in. She saw Imelda kneeling very still. She did not even seem to be breathing.

The Sister went closer; Imelda did not move. The Sister saw that Jesus had taken the little girl with Him to Heaven, because she loved Him so much. After she had received Jesus, she had died.

Blessed Imelda watches over all boys and girls who are going to make their first Holy Communion.

Let us ask her to help us make good Holy Communions. Because Imelda loves Jesus so much, she will help us love Him as we should.

> Imelda's little heart was free from sin.
> How glad she was when Jesus entered in!
> And so I pray that my heart, too, will be
> As pure as hers, when Jesus comes to me.

St. Cyril

One afternoon Paul said to his mother, "To-day Joseph and I came home from school together. Joseph was telling me about the books his big brother James has. He said one of the books tells about people who had to die because they loved God."

"I think Joseph is making a mistake. Such a thing never happened, did it, Mother?"

Paul's mother said, "Yes, it did happen. Long ago many people had to die because they loved God. Even children had to die.

"One of these children was a little boy named Cyril. He lived in a country far across the sea.

"Most of the people in that country did not believe in God. They hated those who did believe in Him. These people were called pagans. Cyril's father was a pagan.

"Cyril himself believed in God and loved Him.

"At first his father did not know this. When he found it out, he beat Cyril. He was cruel to him in many ways. When Cyril said he still loved God, his father drove him out of the house.

"'Go!' he said. 'I will not be your father any longer.'

"Cyril left his home. He wandered about when it was day. At night he slept in the woods. He was never afraid, for he knew God was watching over him. He would say,

"'Dear God, I have a Father who loves me and watches over me. It is You. I have a beautiful home, too. It is Heaven. Dear Father in Heaven, I love You.'

"One day the ruler of the country heard about Cyril. This ruler was a pagan. He grew very angry when he heard how much Cyril loved God. He said to one of the soldiers,

"'Find this boy and bring him to me.'

"Before long, the soldier came back. Cyril was walking bravely beside him. The ruler began to talk to the boy at once.

"He said, 'I will give you money. I will do many fine things for you, too, if you will say you do not believe in God.'

"Cyril looked at the ruler and said, 'I will always believe in God. I will always love Him. I will always love Jesus, who died for us.'

"This made the ruler very angry. He said to himself, 'What shall I do now?' He thought for a while. Then he said, 'I will frighten him. Then he will say what I wish him to say.'

"So Cyril was taken from the room and shown a big fire and a sharp sword. He knew that people who believed in God were sometimes put into such a fire. He knew that sometimes they died by the sword. But these things did not frighten him.

"Cyril was taken back to the ruler. The ruler said, 'You have seen the fire and the sword. Are you ready now to say that you do not believe in God?'

"'No,' said Cyril, 'I will never say that, for I do believe in God. He is my Father and I love Him with all my heart. I want to go to Him.'

"This made the ruler more angry than ever at Cyril. So he had him led away to die by the sword."

When the story was ended, Paul said, "Cyril was very brave, wasn't he, Mother?"

"Yes, he was," said Paul's mother. "He loved God so much he was ready to suffer anything for Him. He is now one of God's saints."

A Lover of Children

One day a number of children were playing near St. Joseph's Church.

An old gentleman with white hair came up to them and said: "May I ask why you are here just now?"

"We are waiting for Father Johnson. He is preparing us for First Holy Communion," was the reply.

All the boys then left their play and came forward to hear what the old gentleman had to say.

"Do you know what Holy Communion is?" asked the old gentleman.

"We all know what Holy Communion is."

"What is Father Johnson going to do this afternoon?"

"He is going to tell us how to make a good confession."

Just then a little girl who had not said a word, asked the gentleman:

"Do you remember when you made your First Holy Communion?"

"I do not remember very much about my First Holy Communion. It was a great many years ago."

"We should like to hear what you remember about it."

"I know that it was the happiest day in my life."

"Did you have your picture taken?" asked another girl.

"Yes, I have it yet. I look at it now and then to remind me of that happy day."

"You must have looked different then," said one of the boys.

"Oh, yes. I had black hair then; now it is white."

For a few minutes, no one spoke. The old gentleman was thinking.

"Though I cannot tell you very much about my First Communion, I know a story about a little boy who made his First Holy Communion in the great city of Rome."

"Is that where the Holy Father lives?" asked one of the boys.

"Yes, my child; that is where the Pope lives."

"Please tell us about the little boy," said the children.

"Not many years ago, a French mother and her two boys took a trip to the city of Rome.

"The older boy was eight years of age, and the younger was six.

"One day, the Holy Father came into a large room to see all the visitors.

"When the mother's time came to speak to the Holy Father, she said to him: 'Holy Father, this little boy hopes to make his First Holy Communion to-morrow morning at your Mass.'

"'And what about the younger boy?' asked the Holy Father.

"'Oh, he is too young to make his First Holy Communion,' replied the mother.

"Drawing the younger boy to him, the Holy Father said: 'Who is it, my child, that you receive in Holy Communion? '

"'The good God,' replied the boy.

"'Would you like to receive your First Holy Communion with your brother? '

"'I should be delighted to do so,' replied the boy.

"The Holy Father then asked him other questions.

"When the little boy answered, the Pope smiled and said:

"'You, too, my dear child, will make your First Holy Communion at my Mass to-morrow morning.'

"'I thank you, Holy Father, you are very kind to me.'

"Then the Pope blessed the French mother and her children."

As the old gentleman finished his story, Father Johnson came. The children thanked the old gentleman and went into the church.

The First Communion

Yes, in that room, the Cenacle,
He took the bread and wine:
And blessed and gave among the Twelve,
And spoke these words divine:
"This is MY BODY; take and eat.
Drink, too MY BLOOD," He said:
"That Flesh which shall be crucified,
That Blood which shall be shed."

The Wonderful Gift

It was the night before Jesus died. He had supper with His friends. These friends of Jesus were His apostles. Jesus had told them that He was about to leave them.

This made the apostles very sad. "What shall we do without Jesus?" they said. "We shall be sad and afraid. We need Jesus."

Jesus was sorry for His apostles. He knew how sad and afraid they were. He knew how much they would need Him.

At the supper, He took bread in His hands. He lifted His eyes to heaven and gave thanks to God, His Father. He blessed the bread. He broke it and gave it to the apostles. Jesus said, "Take ye, and eat. This is My Body."

Then Jesus took wine. He lifted His eyes to heaven and gave thanks to God, His Father. He blessed the wine and gave it to the apostles. Jesus said, "Drink ye all of this. For this is My Blood." So Jesus gave to all of us the wonderful gift, His Body and Blood, the Blessed Sacrament.

O Lord I Am Not Worthy
(O Sacrament Most Holy)

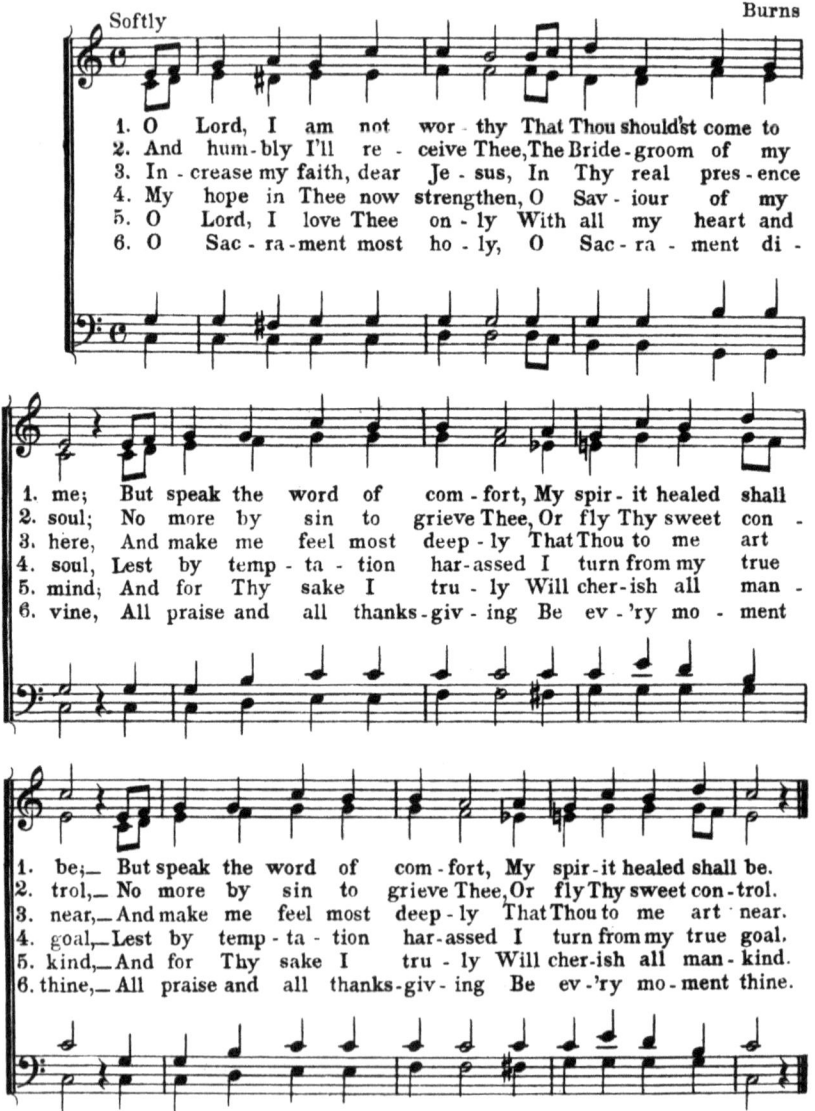

The Child on Calvary

The Cross is tall,
And I too small
To reach His hand
Or touch His feet;
But on the sand
His footprints I have found,
And it is sweet
To kiss the holy ground.

—*Rev. John Banister Tabb*

Nails

Whenever the bright blue nails would drop
Down on the floor of his carpenter shop,
Saint Joseph, prince of carpenter men,
Would stoop to gather them up again;
For he feared for two little sandals sweet,
And very easy to pierce they were
As they pattered over the lumber there
And rode on two little sacred feet.

But alas, on a hill between earth and heaven
One day—two nails in a cross were driven,
And fastened it firm to the sacred feet
Where once rode two little sandals sweet;
And Christ and His mother looked off in death
Afar—to the valley of Nazareth,
Where the carpenter's shop was spread with dust
And the little blue nails, all packed in rust,
Slept in a box on the window-sill;
And Joseph lay sleeping under the hill.

—*Rev. Leonard Feeney, S.J.*

Easter Morning by Heinrich Hofmann

He is Risen

After our dear Lord had suffered and died on the Cross on Good Friday, His friends wrapped His Sacred Body in fine linen, and laid it in a new grave which had been cut out of a rock.

Early the next Sunday morning, some friends of Jesus came to the place where He had been buried. They said to one another: "Who shall roll us back the stone from the door of the grave?"

But when they came to the grave, they saw that the stone had been rolled back, and that the Body of Jesus was not there.

While they were wondering what had happened, an angel said to them: "Be not afraid. You seek Jesus of Nazareth Who was crucified. He is risen. He is not here. Behold the place where they laid Him."

After rising from the dead, Jesus remained forty days on earth. During this time, many people saw Him.

At the end of the forty days, He called together His Apostles and friends. Then lifting up His hands to heaven, He blessed them.

While they looked on, He went up to heaven, where He now sits at the right hand of God.

The First Easter

It was very early in the morning of the first Easter Sunday. Mary Magdalen knelt at the door of Our Lord's tomb. She was crying bitterly. She did not know that Jesus had risen from the dead. She thought that someone had taken His Body away.

The tomb was in a beautiful garden. The flowers were opening, and the birds were singing. But Mary did not see the flowers. She did not hear the birds. She was thinking only of how to find Jesus.

As Mary looked into the tomb she saw two angels sitting, one at the head and one at the feet, where the body of Jesus had been laid.

And the angels said to her, "Woman, why do you weep?"

And Mary answered: "Because they have taken away my Lord. And I do not know where they have laid Him."

Turning away from the tomb, Mary saw Someone standing near. She thought that He was the gardener. He asked: "Woman, why are you weeping? For whom are you looking?"

Mary cried, "Sir, if you have taken Him away from here, tell me where you have laid Him, and I will take Him away."

And Jesus said, " Mary!"

Then Mary knew Him. She knew that the garden was beautiful. She knew that the birds were singing and that the flowers were opening in the sunshine. Jesus had risen from the dead.

Easter had come!

The Resurrection

BUT WHEN three days
   were past and gone,
The stone was rolled away;
And Christ the King,
   triumphantly,
Came forth on Easter day.
O sing the song of glory
That He who came to save,
The Son of God,
   Our Master, Lord,
Is risen from the grave!

Frank's First Confession

On beautiful summer day, some years ago, a number of little boys were playing ball in a large field.

At the end of the ninth inning, the score was four to four. So it took another inning to finish the game.

At the close of the next inning, the score was six to four.

Shortly after this, the boys began to quarrel about the game.

They called each other names; and one of them became angry and took the Holy Name of Jesus in vain.

The other boys were shocked. They told him that it was a great sin.

When Frank went home that evening, he was very sad.

"What is the matter, my child?" asked the mother. "Did some of the big boys hit you, my son?"

"No, mother; no one did anything to me. I did it myself."

"And what did you do, my boy?"

Frank then told his mother about the quarrel, and how he used the Holy Name of Jesus.

"The big boys said, mother, that it is a sin, and that I ought to get it off my soul as soon as I can."

Frank's mother tried to comfort him. She said to him: "God will forgive you, my child, if you are truly sorry for what you have done, and if you tell the sin in confession."

"But I do not know how to go to confession, mother."

"I will tell you all about it after supper, my dear."

After preparing for a few weeks, Father Summers told him that he knew enough to go to confession.

The next Friday afternoon, Frank and his mother went to the church.

After saying his prayers for a short time, Frank went into the confessional.

He told all his sins, and the number of times of each sin, to the priest; and he said that he was very sorry for them.

The priest spoke kindly to the boy, and gave him absolution.

When Frank came out of the confessional, he was no longer sad. A sweet smile lighted up his face.

He went to the altar, and thanked the dear Jesus for having taken away his sins. Then he said from his heart: "I will never again take Your Holy Name in vain, dear Jesus."

O
Come,
Holy Spirit,
Come down from above,
Of our hearts for King Jesus
Make cradles of
Love.

Come, Holy Ghost

Saint Peter

Our Lord had twelve apostles. They were all good men but one. They loved our Lord, and He loved them very much.

Saint Peter was one of the twelve apostles. He liked to work for Jesus. He loved him very much.

The night before Our Lord died He ate the Last Supper with His apostles.

After supper He told them that He was going away. Peter wanted to go with Him.

He said to Jesus, "I will go with You and die with You!"

But Jesus said to him, "Before the cock crows in the morning you will say three times that you do not know Me."

After supper Jesus went into a garden to pray. The apostles went with Him, but they fell asleep. Jesus prayed alone.

When the men came to take Jesus away, Peter struck one of them with his sword. He cut off the man's ear.

But Jesus said: "Peter, put your sword away. It is time for Me to die."

So the men took Jesus away.

Then Peter began to be afraid. He did not know how to help Jesus. He did not know what to do. He saw the men take Jesus away. He walked after them very slowly and very sadly.

They took Jesus to a big hall. Peter went into the hall, too.

Soon a girl came up to him. She said, "Oh! You are one of the twelve good friends of Jesus!"

Then Peter was afraid and cried, "No! I am not His friend!" And he walked away.

Another girl came up to Peter. "You know Jesus," she said.

"No!" cried Peter. "I do not know Him!"

Soon a man said to him:

"I saw you with Jesus. You are one of the twelve."

Peter cried, "No! No! You did not see me! I do not know the Man!"

Just then a cock crowed. And Jesus looked at Peter.

Peter went out of the hall. He went out into the dark.

The big tears ran down his face. He cried: "O my God, forgive me! I did not love Jesus! I said I did not know Him! Forgive my sin!"

God forgave Peter.

He told him to take care of the Church. He made him the first Pope.

But Saint Peter never forgot that he had sinned. He was always kind to sinners.

Long Live the Pope

190

4. Then raise the chant with heart and voice
In church and school and home,
Long live the Shepherd of the Flock,
Long live the Pope of Rome.
Almighty Father, bless his work,
Protect him in his ways,
Receive his prayers, fulfil his hopes
And grant him length of days.

Saint Felix and the Spider

Long ago in the sunny land of Italy there lived a holy bishop named Felix.

Felix was a saint, and all the Christians loved him dearly because he was so good and kind to them.

Now, at that time, the Romans did not like the Christians. They often put them to death because they believed in Christ.

Many of the Christians left Rome and went to a far country so they could live in peace.

St. Felix was old and weak, but he would not go away.

He said, "I cannot leave my people. I am their father, and I must stay near them when they are in trouble."

So St. Felix put on the dress of a traveler and, taking a staff in his hand, he went to see the frightened Christians in their homes.

One day, as the old man was walking down the street, he met a band of fierce soldiers.

"Ho, old traveler!" said the captain of the soldiers as he pulled out his sword, "we are looking for Felix, the bishop. We went to his home, but he was not there. Have you met him on the way? If you do not tell me the truth, you shall lose your head."

St. Felix looked into the captain's eyes and said, "I have met no one in an hour."

St. Felix spoke the truth, for he had passed no one on the way, and, if he had done so, it would not have been himself.

So the soldiers let the old man pass, and they went off quickly to search on another road.

St. Felix hurried away, too, for he knew that the soldiers would soon find out that he had played a trick on them. He had walked but a short distance when he heard once more the shouts of the soldiers. He heard their loud cries and the noise of their swords, and he knew they were following him again.

The poor old man was tired and out of breath. He was too weak to run, so he looked about for a hiding place. By the side of the road he saw an old

stone wall. In this wall was a large hole. St. Felix crawled into the hole. It was a poor hiding place, but it was the best he could find.

"Save me, dear Lord, for the sake of the poor Christians, Thy children," prayed St. Felix as he knelt down on the hard stones.

That minute, St. Felix's prayer was answered.

A little spider came tumbling down from the wall outside and began to spin its web across the hole. Back and forth, to and fro, up and down, it went as quick as lightning. From one side to another it jumped and crawled and ran, and soon it had spun a heavy web. Then the wind came up and blew the dust from the roadside upon the web.

"Now," said St. Felix, "I have a fine curtain at my window. I cannot even see out. Thank you, little spider, for your kind deed. I think you have saved my life."

Just then the soldiers came to the wall.

"Here is a hole in the wall!" cried one. "Do you think the old man can be in there?"

"You foolish fellow!" said the captain. "Do you not see that old spider web? How could any one have crawled into the hole without breaking the web?"

"No one has been in there for many and many a day," said another soldier. "We are but wasting time. Come, let us go on."

Then the soldiers walked away, leaving St. Felix safe.

That night St. Felix came out from his hiding place and went to live in an old well. A good Christian woman found him there, and every day, for a long, long time, she brought him food and drink.

At last, the Romans let the poor Christians live in peace. Then St. Felix left the well and went back to his people. How glad they were to see him, and how they thanked God for sparing his life!

—Catholic Folklore

Jerome and the Lion

I

One fine morning Jerome was driving a little donkey along the bank of a river. On the little donkey's back was a large jar of water, for they had just been down to the river to get water for dinner.

Now Jerome was a holy monk, and he lived with many other monks in a large house on the hill.

The sun was very hot, but the birds in the trees were singing sweetly. So, as Jerome walked along, he, too, began to sing.

All at once he heard a strange sound. It was not a bird's song. It was too loud for that. The little donkey stopped and, throwing up his ears, stood still, looking very much frightened. Jerome stopped, too. But he was not afraid, for he was too good. Still, he wondered at the sound.

"Dear me!" he said. "What a very strange sound! What do you suppose it was?" Of course, he was talking to himself, for no one else was near.

Jerome looked around, but he saw nothing, so he started once more up the hill. He had gone but a few steps when the sound came again. This time it was a sad sound, and it stopped with a whine.

The donkey trembled all over, he was so frightened. His master said, "It must be a lion."

And a lion it was. Just at that minute the great head and the yellow eyes of a lion appeared among the bushes beside the road. Then, giving his sad cry again, the lion jumped out and came toward good Jerome, who was holding the donkey tight to keep him from running away.

He was a very large lion, much larger than the donkey. As he came near, Jerome saw that he was lame. At once the good man was sorry for the poor animal, because he did not like to see any of God's creatures suffer. He went to meet the lion, and put his hand on his head.

The lion did not jump at Jerome or try to kill him, but he lay down at his feet and began to whine.

"Poor old fellow!" said Jerome. "What makes you lame, Brother Lion?"

The lion shook his head and roared. But his eyes were not fierce. They looked up at Jerome as if asking him for help. Then the lion held up his right front paw and shook it, to show that this was the lame foot.

"Lie down, sir," said Jerome, just as you would talk to a big dog.

The lion lay down, and Jerome took up his great paw in his hand. Then he saw a long thorn. No wonder the poor lion had roared and whined in pain.

As Jerome took out the thorn, the lion did not make a sound. When the thorn was out, the lion looked up into the monk's face as if he wanted to say, "Thank you, kind friend, I will not forget."

II

Again Jerome and the donkey began to climb the hill for home. As he walked along, Jerome heard the sound of soft steps behind him. He turned round and saw that the great lion was following him.

"Suppose he goes all the way home with me," thought Jerome to himself. "What shall I do with him?"

When he reached home, he took the jar of water from the donkey's back. Then he put the donkey into the stable.

As he turned to go into the house, the lion lay down at his feet and pulled at his gown with his paws, as if to say, "Kind friend, I love you because you took the thorn out of my foot. Let me stay with you always."

Jerome said, "You may stay as long as you are good."

Then he walked into the house. The lion went behind him and lay down on the floor like a kitten, and soon he went to sleep.

III

Wherever Jerome went, Leo, the lion, went also. Best of all, Leo liked to go to the river for water. As the donkey walked along with the jar of water on his back, Leo would run and jump on the sand and have great fun.

One day as Jerome was on the way to the river with the donkey and the lion, a poor man ran out to him and asked him to come into his hut and cure his sick baby.

Of course, Jerome was glad to go with the poor man. But before he went, he said, "Stay here, Leo, and watch the donkey."

Now, Leo wished to obey his master, but the day was hot, and he was sleepy. He lay on the sand beside the donkey and tried to keep his eyes open, but, before he knew it, he was asleep.

The foolish donkey soon grew tired of standing beside the sleeping lion, so off he went to get a bite of green grass. As he ate, he walked farther and farther away from the lion.

By and by a camel driver came along with a band of horses and camels and donkeys. He was taking them to a country far away.

"What a fine little donkey!" he cried. "I shall take him along with me."

With that, the camel driver took the water jar off the donkey's back and then drove the donkey away in front of him.

Now the noise woke Leo. He jumped up with a roar just in time to see the camel driver's face as he

went over the hill. But he did not see the donkey. Around and around he ran, smelling the air, but he could not find his friend. Then he stood by the water jar and roared with all his might.

When Jerome came out and saw Leo standing beside the water jar. and found that the donkey was gone, he thought Leo had eaten him.

"You wicked lion!" he cried. "You have eaten my poor donkey. What shall I do?"

But Leo only roared louder. He could not talk and tell his master what had happened.

Jerome was very sad. "You will have to be my donkey now," he said. "Come, stand up, and let me tie the water jar upon your back."

Leo hung his head and stood still while the good monk tied the water jar upon his back. He was ashamed to do a donkey's work, for he was the

King of Beasts. He was sadder still to think that his master was angry with him.

When they reached home, Jerome told the story to the other monks. They, too, said that Leo would have to take the donkey's place and go for water every day.

This was a sad time for Leo. He could no longer sleep in the house, but had to be tied in the stable. How he wished that he could talk and tell his master that he had done no wrong! But he was only a lion, and all he could do was roar or whine.

Many months passed by. Leo was still doing the donkey's work.

One day Jerome took Leo to a little town. The good man wished to buy food in the town. Then he would tie it upon Leo's back, and Leo would carry it home.

Jerome bought the food and was putting it into baskets when he heard Leo give a loud growl. Looking up, he saw a long train of horses, camels, and donkeys going by.

Leo had seen the face of the camel driver, and he knew the man was the one who had taken the poor donkey.

The lion ran toward the camel driver, but as he went he saw his old friend, the donkey.

With a roar and a jump he caught at the donkey's bridle and led the poor frightened animal to Jerome.

Then Jerome knew the truth. He looked at the donkey well. While he did so, the lion looked up at him and growled as if to say, "Here is your old donkey, safe and sound. You see I did not eat him after all. There is the real thief." And, turning toward the camel driver, the lion roared and looked so fierce that the poor man ran away as fast as he could go.

"This is my donkey," the good monk said, "and I shall take him home with me."

Then he tied the baskets upon the donkey, who was happy to be once more with his old master.

"My poor old Leo!" said Jerome. "I have not been kind to you, but now I know you are faithful."

Then the three set out for home, and all the way Jerome kept his hand upon the lion's head.

How happy Leo was to know that he and his dear master were friends once more!

Leo lived with the good monk for many, many years, and he was always a good and faithful friend.

— *Catholic Folklore*

The String of Beads

Little Therese wanted to be good. Every day she tried very hard to be good. Every night she asked her big sister: "Have I been good today? Is God pleased with me?"

One day Therese's sister gave her some beads. They were on a string.

Her sister said: "Therese, this string of beads is for you. You like to count. Now you can count on these beads the good things you do every day."

Therese thanked her sister. It was fun to count the beads. The string of beads helped her, too. It helped her to be good.

Every night Therese counted her good deeds on her string of beads. If there were many, she was glad.

She said, "Today Our Lord was pleased with me."

But if there were only a few she said: "Dear Jesus, I am sorry. I will do better tomorrow. Please help me! I want to be good. I love You!"

Our Lord did help her. He helped her to grow better every day. After Therese died, she was made a saint.

Playing Saints

Therese and Marie were coming home from school. They were walking very slowly. They were talking about school.

Jane said: "Come, little girls, you are slow tonight. We shall be late. You must walk faster."

So Therese and Marie walked faster. They walked very, very fast. Then they began to run.

Soon Jane was far behind.

Therese said: "Marie, let us play that we are saints! Let us walk like this!"

Therese shut her eyes. She began to say her rosary.

Marie shut her eyes. She began to say her rosary.

The two little saints walked on and on and on. Their eyes were shut. They walked very slowly.

Before long they came to a store. There were many big boxes in front of the store. There were little boxes, too.

The saints came to the boxes. They did not see them. Do you know what happened?

Bump! Down came the boxes and down came the saints. Two little girls opened their eyes. They picked themselves up. They ran home.

The storekeeper came out to see what had happened. He was very cross.

He said: "Look at my boxes! Look at them!" But Therese and Marie were far away.

When Jane came to the store she saw what had happened. She felt sorry for the storekeeper. She helped to pick up the boxes.

When she got home, she was cross. The two little girls cried and cried. They told her how it had happened. They were very much frightened. They were sorry too.

Jane said: "You were very silly. Saints do not shut their eyes on the street. They keep them open. They help others. They pray at the right time. They love God all the time!"

Mary's Smile

The Little Flower was very ill. She had been ill for a long time. The doctors said that she was dying.

Therese's father said, "Let us ask Our Blessed Mother to help her." So nine Masses were said. And everybody prayed for nine days.

It was Sunday, and Therese was so ill that she did not know her father. She could not see her sisters.

Everybody was praying to Our Blessed Mother to help the poor little sick girl.

Suddenly Therese opened her eyes and looked at her statue of Blessed Mother. She cried, "O Mother! Have pity on me!"

It seemed to Therese that the statue was really Our Blessed Mother. She looked at Therese with a beautiful smile, and just then the pain went away and Therese began to get better. She was soon well.

Sleep Song

Sleep, child of mine, in safety now,
God's holy sign is on your brow,
God's holy angels, brave and bright,
Will guard your slumber through the night.

Sleep, child of mine, in safety sleep,
God's holy ones their watch will keep,
And from your side they will not rise
Till dawn again lights up the skies.

—Denis A. McCarthy

www.ingramcontent.com/pod-product-compliance
Lightning Source LLC
Chambersburg PA
CBHW042145160426
43202CB00022B/2985